New York Times v. Sullivan

Affirming Freedom of the Press

Harvey Fireside

Landmark Supreme Court Cases

Enslow Publishers, Inc.

44 Fadem Road	PO Box 38
Box 699	Aldershot
Springfield, NJ 07081	Hants GU12 6BP
USA	UK

http://www.enslow.com

To Daniel and Lisa

Library of Congress Cataloging-in-Publication Data

Fireside, Harvey.
    New York Times v. Sullivan: Affirming freedom of the press / Harvey Fireside.
        p. cm. — (Landmark Supreme Court cases)
    Includes bibliographical references and index.
    Summary: Describes the Supreme Court decision in the case of New York Times v.
Sullivan, preventing public officials from receiving damages for false statements unless
they can prove actual malice.
    ISBN 0-7660-1085-6
    1. Sullivan, L. B. —Trials, litigation, etc. —Juvenile literature. 2. New York Times
Company—Trials, litigation, etc.—Juvenile literature. 3. Trials (Libel)—Alabama—
Montgomery—Juvenile literature. 4. Freedom of the press—United States—Juvenile
literature. 5. Libel and slander—United States—Juvenile literature. [1. Sullivan, L. B.—
Trials, litigation, etc. 2. New York Times Company—Trials, litigation, etc. 3. Freedom of
the press. 4. Civil rights.] I. Title. II. Series.
KF228.N4F57   1999
342.73'0853—dc21   98-36959
                                             CIP
                                             AC

To Our Readers:
All Internet addresses in this book were active and appropriate when we went to press. Any
comments or suggestions can be sent by e-mail to Comments@enslow.com or to the address
on the back cover.

Photo Credits: Harris and Ewing, Collection of the Supreme Court of the United
States, pp. 83, 95; Ken Heinen, Collection of the Supreme Court of the United
States, p. 80; Library of Congress, pp. 13, 18, 24, 26, 28, 41, 42, 56, 57, 78, 101,
106; Library of Congress, *U.S. News & World Report* magazine collection, p. 32;
National Archives, p. 37; *The New York Times*, p. 9; Painting by Gilbert Stuart,
Reproduced from the *Dictionary of American Portraits* published by Dover
Publications, Inc., 1967, p. 68; Painting by Gilbert Stuart, Courtesy of Bowdoin
College Museum of Art, Reproduced from the *Dictionary of American Portraits*
published by Dover Publications, Inc., 1967, p. 46.

Cover Photos: Franz Jantzen, "Collection of the Supreme Court of the United
States (background); Library of Congress (crowd protest inset), National Archives
(Dr. Martin Luther King, Jr. inset).

Contents

1

A Clash in Montgomery

In March 1960, thousands of African-American students were demonstrating in the South. They were trying to assert their basic rights. They wanted to be able to vote without undue restrictions, to be treated fairly by the police and by the courts, and to attend public schools (which until then had been set aside for whites). These were all rights guaranteed by the Constitution. These rights had also been upheld by the Supreme Court of the United States. Yet southern governors, mayors, sheriffs, and school boards refused to change the existing system of racial segregation.

For example, the Supreme Court's historic 1954 *Brown* v. *Board of Education* decision prohibited separate public schooling for black and for white children. Yet it took nearly a decade before public schools in the

South even began to offer equal education to all children. By 1960, only some northern and border states had obeyed the unanimous opinion of the Court. Only one sixth of one percent of black students in the South went to a desegregated school.[1] In the heart of the South—Alabama and Mississippi—not one single class in any public school had been integrated.

Young people had launched what is called the civil rights movement that same year. On Monday, February 1, 1960, four freshmen from North Carolina Agricultural and Technical College staged the first sit-in. A *sit-in* is a demonstration in which protesters sit down and refuse to move until their needs are addressed. Joseph McNeill, Ezell Blair, Jr., Franklin McCain, and David Richmond went to the lunch counter of Woolworth's department store in downtown Greensboro, North Carolina. The waitress explained that this counter was for "whites only." They would have to move to the "colored" counter before she could serve them. They refused to move and waited for their coffee and doughnuts until the store closed.[2]

The African-American students were back the next day. On Tuesday, the four students had been joined by twenty-three others. By the end of the week, their number had grown to three hundred. Soon thousands of them conducted boycotts of this and other stores, vowing not to shop there until they were served equally. Other demonstrators staged sit-ins in Raleigh, North Carolina; High Point, Virginia; and Tallahassee, Florida. Students from nearby white colleges also arrived to lend their support.

These protests were nonviolent. The African-American students relied on sit-ins, picket lines, and marches to get their message across. But the reaction from their white neighbors often turned violent. At the Woolworth's in Nashville, Tennessee, the backs of girls sitting at the counter were burned by white hecklers holding cigarettes. The hecklers spat at the demonstrators and pelted them with french fries and gum. Yet the police arrested only the peaceful demonstrators, not their attackers. In Orangeburg, South Carolina, a march in support of the sit-ins was met by police with tear gas and high-pressure fire hoses. Hundreds of the soaked students were held in jails, some of them shivering in a chicken coop turned into a prison cell.

On February 25, thirty-five students from Alabama State College sat in at the snack bar of the courthouse in Montgomery, Alabama. Governor John Patterson ordered the college president to expel any students who had been involved. The governor was also chairman of the state's board of education. A campus rally was addressed by Martin Luther King, Jr., the minister of

Ebenezer Baptist Church in Atlanta. The students pledged to drop out of school if any of them were expelled. The Reverend Ralph Abernathy led a prayer meeting for about eight hundred protesters on the steps of the state capitol.[3]

The Advertisement in *The New York Times*

One month later, a full-page advertisement appeared in *The New York Times*. The March 29 issue carried an appeal entitled, "Heed Their Rising Voices," on behalf of the student protesters and Dr. King. It began by saying, "As the whole world knows by now, thousands of Southern Negro students are engaged in widespread nonviolent demonstrations in positive affirmation of the right to live in human dignity as guaranteed by the U.S. Constitution and the Bill of Rights." Ten paragraphs of small type described actions of the students and Dr. King. The text ended with an appeal for funds that would be used for three purposes: (1) to support the student movement; (2) for the legal defense of Dr. Martin Luther King, then under an indictment for perjury in Montgomery; and (3) to aid "the struggle for the right-to-vote."

This advertisement would eventually lead to a major Supreme Court case known as *New York Times* v. *Sullivan*. L. B. Sullivan was one of the three commissioners who formed the city government of Montgomery. Although

THE NEW YORK TIMES, TUESDAY, MARCH 29, 1960.   L   25

"The growing movement of peaceful mass demonstrations by Negroes is something new in the South, something understandable.... Let Congress heed their rising voices, for they will be heard."

—New York Times editorial
Saturday, March 19, 1960

Heed Their Rising Voices

As the whole world knows by now, thousands of Southern Negro students are engaged in widespread non-violent demonstrations in positive affirmation of the right to live in human dignity as guaranteed by the U. S. Constitution and the Bill of Rights. In their efforts to uphold these guarantees, they are being met by an unprecedented wave of terror by those who would deny and negate that document which the whole world looks upon as setting the pattern for modern freedom....

In Orangeburg, South Carolina, when 400 students peacefully sought to buy doughnuts and coffee at lunch counters in the business district, they were forcibly ejected, tear-gassed, soaked to the skin in freezing weather with fire hoses, arrested en masse and herded into an open barbed-wire stockade to stand for hours in the bitter cold.

In Montgomery, Alabama, after students sang "My Country, 'Tis of Thee" on the State Capitol steps, their leaders were expelled from school, and truckloads of police armed with shotguns and tear-gas ringed the Alabama State College Campus. When the entire student body protested to state authorities by refusing to re-register, their dining hall was padlocked in an attempt to starve them into submission.

In Tallahassee, Atlanta, Nashville, Savannah, Greensboro, Memphis, Richmond, Charlotte, and a host of other cities in the South, young American teen-agers, in face of the entire weight of official state apparatus and police power, have boldly stepped forth as protagonists of democracy. Their courage and amazing restraint have inspired millions and given a new dignity to the cause of freedom.

Small wonder that the Southern violators of the Constitution fear this new, non-violent brand of freedom fighter ... even as they fear the upwelling right-to-vote movement. Small wonder that they are determined to destroy the one man who, more than any other, symbolizes the new spirit now sweeping the South—the Rev. Dr. Martin Luther King, Jr., world-famous leader of the Montgomery Bus Protest. For it is his doctrine of non-violence which has inspired and guided the students in their widening wave of sit-ins; and it is this same Dr. King who founded and is president of the Southern Christian Leadership Conference—the organization which is spearheading the surging right-to-vote movement. Under Dr. King's direction the Leadership Conference conducts Student Workshops and Seminars in the philosophy and technique of non-violent resistance.

Again and again the Southern violators have answered Dr. King's peaceful protests with intimidation and violence. They have bombed his home almost killing his wife and child. They have assaulted his person. They have arrested him seven times—for "speeding," "loitering" and similar "offenses." And now they have charged him with "perjury"—a felony under which they could imprison him for ten years. Obviously, their real purpose is to remove him physically as the leader to whom the students and millions of others—look for guidance and support, and thereby to intimidate all leaders who may rise in the South. Their strategy is to behead this affirmative movement, and thus to demoralize Negro Americans and weaken their will to struggle. The defense of Martin Luther King, spiritual leader of the student sit-in movement, clearly, therefore, is an integral part of the total struggle for freedom in the South.

Decent-minded Americans cannot help but applaud the creative daring of the students and the quiet heroism of Dr. King. But this is one of those moments in the stormy history of Freedom when men and women of good will must do more than applaud the rising-to-glory of others. The America whose good name hangs in the balance before a watchful world, the America whose heritage of Liberty these Southern Upholders of the Constitution are defending, is our America as well as theirs ...

We must heed their rising voices—yes—but we must add our own.

We must extend ourselves above and beyond moral support and render the material help so urgently needed by those who are taking the risks, facing jail, and even death in a glorious re-affirmation of our Constitution and its Bill of Rights.

We urge you to join hands with our fellow Americans in the South by supporting, with your dollars, this Combined Appeal for all three needs—the defense of Martin Luther King—the support of the embattled students—and the struggle for the right-to-vote.

Your Help Is Urgently Needed . . . NOW ! !

We in the south who are struggling daily for dignity and freedom warmly endorse this appeal

Please mail this coupon TODAY!

COMMITTEE TO DEFEND MARTIN LUTHER KING AND THE STRUGGLE FOR FREEDOM IN THE SOUTH
312 West 125th Street, New York 27, N. Y. UNiversity 6-1700

Chairmen: A. Philip Randolph, Dr. Gardner C. Taylor; Treasurer: Nat King Cole; Executive Director: Bayard Rustin; Chairmen of Cultural Division: Harry Belafonte, Sidney Poitier; Chairman of Church Division: Father George B. Ford, Rev. Harry Emerson Fosdick, Rev. Thomas Kilgore, Jr., Rabbi Edward E. Klein; Chairman of Labor Division: Morris Iushewitz

This full-page advertisement appeared in *The New York Times* on March 29, 1960. The text describes the actions of student protesters and Dr. Martin Luther King and ends with an appeal for funds.

his name had not appeared in the ad, Sullivan said that he had been injured by it. As the person in charge of the city police, he brought suit against *The New York Times* and four African-American ministers in Montgomery who had signed the ad, along with other clergymen and about sixty well-known people headed by Eleanor Roosevelt, widow of President Franklin D. Roosevelt.

This case began on November 1, 1960, with a jury trial in a state court in Montgomery. *The New York Times* was charged with libel. Sullivan, the plaintiff, claimed that the newspaper, as well as the ministers, had injured his reputation. He was trying to collect money damages to compensate him. One frequent defense to this charge is for a publisher to show the truth of what had been printed. In the Montgomery trial, however, the *Times* admitted that the ad contained a number of false statements. That allowed the judge to tell the jury that the fact of libel had been established. All that was left for them to do was affirm it in a verdict for Sullivan and determine how much money to pay in damages.

There were three aspects of the trial that may have shocked readers who learned about it from the *Times* and other newspapers. First, the courtroom atmosphere was quite obviously racist. Second, Sullivan asked for $500,000 damages in his suit, even though he had not shown any loss caused by the ad. Third, the large sum the *Times* would have to pay was clearly a signal to the media from the North. From then on, the media would have to choose each word carefully when reporting on southern protests.

Racist Courtroom Atmosphere

Walter Burgwyn Jones, the judge who presided over the trial, had written *The Confederate Creed*. This publication supported the southern way of life before the Civil War. In it, Jones said, "with unfaltering trust in the God of my fathers, I believe, as a Confederate, in obedience to Him; it is my duty to respect the laws and ancient ways of my people, and to stand up for the right of my state to determine what is good for its people in all local affairs."[4] This was a message to show Judge Jones's opposition to the Supreme Court's decision in *Brown* v. *Board of Education*. At the trial in Montgomery, the judge did not allow black and white spectators to sit together. He said that "in keeping with the common law of Alabama, and observing the wise, time-honored customs and usages of our people . . . there will be no integrated seating in this courtroom."[5] T. Eric Embry, the Birmingham attorney defending *The New York Times*, questioned this ruling on constitutional grounds. Judge Jones countered that the Fourteenth Amendment (guaranteeing due process and equal protection to all people) had "no standing whatever in this court, it is a pariah and an outcast."[6]

Judge Jones also showed his racism in other ways. He addressed the lawyers for Sullivan and *The New York Times* as "Mister." But he called the African-American lawyers defending the four black ministers simply "Lawyer Crawford, Lawyer Gray and Lawyer Seay." Vernon Z. Crawford also objected to Sullivan's lawyer, Calvin Whitesell, mispronouncing the word *Negro*. He said to the judge, "we would like to object to the reading of that ad unless the counsel who reads it will read what is said and as I recall from reading that ad there is nothing on there that is spelled 'n-i-g-g-e-r-s.' It is spelled 'N-e-g-r-o' and I am sure he is well aware of it." The judge did nothing to respond to this objection. The offending lawyer made no excuse. He said, "I have been pronouncing it that way all my life."[7]

Judge Jones also made rulings that were generally favorable to Sullivan's case. For example, in his opening briefs, defense attorney Embry moved to reject the complaint. The newspaper was incorporated in New York, he argued, not subject to Alabama courts. The *Times* sold only 394 of its 650,000 daily papers in that state. Embry was careful to say that he was only making a "special appearance" (for this sole purpose) to make the motion. That was in accord with a manual on the

The judge in the *New York Times* v. *Sullivan* case in Montgomery, Alabama, supported the separation of blacks and whites. This photo shows a time when separate drinking fountains for whites and blacks were common in the South.

state's judicial procedure written by Judge Jones. The judge, however, ruled that Embry was making a "general appearance." That meant—in spite of the judge's own manual—he had trapped Embry. By appearing in the state's court, the lawyer, and through him the *Times*, had, in fact, acknowledged its authority.[8]

The four African-American ministers asked that the suit against them be dropped. They submitted sworn statements saying their names had appeared in the ad without their permission or even their knowledge. Sullivan's lawyers offered no evidence to dispute this. The names of the ministers had evidently been included in the ad because their churches had ties to the Southern Christian Leadership Conference. Yet Judge Jones refused to drop the four ministers from the list of defendants.[9]

The judge also permitted photographs and videos of the jury to be taken in the courtroom. Jury members appeared by name in the newspapers and on television. Because of resulting pressure from their neighbors, the *Times* claimed, the jury members could not be "fair and impartial."[10]

The reporting of the case in the local media was biased against the *Times* from the beginning. An editorial in the *Montgomery Advertiser* on April 7, 1960, began,

> There are voluntary liars. There are involuntary liars. Both kinds of liars contributed to the crude slanders against Montgomery broadcast in a full-page advertisement in *The New York Times* March 29. And it's up to *The New York Times* and the involuntary liars to purge themselves of their false witness."[11]

The lawyers for Sullivan also used racist themes. One of them said in his closing argument to the jury: "All of these things that happened didn't happen in Russia where the police run everything; they didn't happen in the Congo where they still eat 'em. They happened in Montgomery, a law-abiding community."[12]

Half Million Dollars in Damages Requested

Sullivan was asking for half a million dollars in damages, though he had not even been named in the ad. His lawyers argued that the ad charged the Montgomery police with actions harming the Alabama State College students and Martin Luther King, Jr. They said that Sullivan's reputation had been damaged, because he was known to be the city official in charge of the police (as well as the fire department, the office for scales, and the cemetery). They called six witnesses, including several friends of Sullivan. These six men said that they would have thought badly of him if they had believed the statements in the ad. On cross-examination, however, they admitted that they did not believe what the ad said. Therefore, they did not really think worse of Sullivan.

Embry, the *Times* attorney, tried to show that Sullivan was not hurt at all by the ad. Indeed, it probably helped his career to be criticized in a well-known New York newspaper. In his cross-examination, Embry asked, "Have you ever been ridiculed?" Sullivan answered, "I haven't had anyone come up to me personally and say they held me in ridicule because of the ad." Embry continued, "Has anyone threatened to have you removed from office?" The answer was, "No." "Have you been shunned by anyone in a public place?" Sullivan said, "I don't recall."[13]

Still, Sullivan had Alabama libel law on his side. For example, he had followed the law by asking the *Times* to print a corrected version of the ad before he filed his libel suit. The newspaper investigated and found a number of errors in the ad, but answered Sullivan that it found the text "substantially correct." The paper also told him it was "somewhat puzzled as to how you think the statements in any way reflect on you."[14] It never made an apology to Sullivan, although it had printed a correction on behalf of Alabama governor John Patterson. The paper said the apology was owed the governor as "the embodiment of the state" who was in charge of officials who were criticized in the ad.

Sullivan never responded to the *Times*'s request for specifics. But his lawyers argued that, as city commissioner for the police, he was hurt by any mention in the ad of police misconduct. The attorneys stretched this link very far. In court, they said that it connected Sullivan to the police who had repeatedly arrested Martin Luther King. It even made him seem to be one of the "southern violators" who, according to the ad, had bombed Reverend Martin Luther King's house, "almost killing his wife and child," assaulted him, and charged him with perjury (lying under oath). All these actions—though they took place long before Sullivan became a commissioner—could be taken as "imputing improper conduct to him, and subjecting him to public contempt, ridicule and shame."[15]

Judge Jones directed the outcome of the trial by telling the jury that the controversial parts of the ad were "libelous per se," that is, they would obviously hurt the reputation of anyone they described. Under state law, that meant the statements were to be considered false. The only defense for the *Times* was to prove that they were completely accurate. But a number of (mostly minor) mistakes had already been admitted by the *Times*. Finally, the judge told the jury that Sullivan did not have to offer any evidence of being injured. If the jury members agreed that the *Times* had printed the ad and that it referred to Sullivan, they could decide how much money he would be awarded. Sullivan's lawyer had concluded his speech to the jury by saying, "One way to get their attention is to hit them [newspapers] in the pocketbook."[16]

The Northern Media Gets a Signal

The jury took only two hours to find the *Times* and the four ministers guilty of libel. The jury decided that each of the five defendants owed Sullivan $500,000 in damages. It was a combination of ordinary damages—for

L. B. Sullivan's lawyers claimed Sullivan was due an apology because the advertisement in *The New York Times* connected Sullivan to the police who had repeatedly arrested Martin Luther King (shown at left).

injuring his reputation—and punitive damages—for falsehoods that were intended to do harm. (Ordinary damages are supposed to make up for an injury; punitive damages are meant to keep others from committing similar acts.) None of the evidence had shown that Sullivan's standing in his community had been hurt. Nor had staff members of the *Times* admitted anything but carelessness in checking the facts before the ad was published. In law, this is not as serious as deliberate intent to harm. And as has been stated already, there was no proof in court that the four ministers even knew anything about the ad until they were sued.

The court's message was spelled out in the next day's newspapers. The *Montgomery Advertiser* announced the decision in a headline saying, "$500,000 Damages Awarded Sullivan by *Times* Suit."[17] When the Alabama supreme court affirmed the decision, the Advertiser announced, "State Finds Formidable Legal Club to Swing at Out-of-State Press."[18] In other words, northern reporters and their newspapers were put on notice. If they wrote false articles that were critical of southern officials, they might have to pay huge sums in libel judgments.

The half-million dollar award was not the end of it. In a criminal trial there is a rule against "double jeopardy," that is, being charged twice for the same offense. However, this libel case was a civil trial. Double jeopardy did not apply. The other two commissioners of the city of Montgomery, therefore, could file separate libel suits against the *Times*. They soon did, and they were joined by Governor Patterson despite the public apology he had asked for and received from the editors. Even a corporation like *The New York Times* could not afford the millions that it was sentenced to pay in this suit and in others that followed. It pressed on with appeals all the way to the United States Supreme Court.

The Montgomery court had not only cracked the whip over newspapers that dared to challenge the segregated society of the South, but also threatened to cut off northern support for the civil rights movement. Southern protesters needed national attention to overcome racism. Only then could they recruit enough volunteers and obtain sufficient funds to carry on their struggle. If they remained a regional effort, they were not likely to persuade Congress and the president to adopt new civil rights laws or to enforce existing laws and court decisions.

At one level, *New York Times* v. *Sullivan* was merely about libel laws. The courts had to decide whether or not the fifty states could define libel law. Or should there be a new federal standard to serve as a guideline under the First Amendment? At a more immediate level, this case affected the African Americans fighting against segregation in the South. Would the threat of huge money penalties frighten them into silence?

2

Civil Rights at the Crossroads

At the time of the libel trial against *The New York Times* and the four African-American ministers in Montgomery, the civil rights movement was at a crossroads. Four major groups were active in 1960. One of them was the chief target of Sullivan's lawsuit.

National Association for the Advancement of Colored People (NAACP)

The oldest and best-known civil rights organization is the National Association for the Advancement of Colored People (NAACP). It was founded in 1910. Thurgood Marshall, who headed its Legal Defense Fund, had won a series of legal victories. African-American students were being admitted to a few southern universities, but almost none to public schools in the South. Politicians and local judges were not fulfilling the 1954 mandate of the Supreme Court in *Brown* v. *Board of Education.* They were determined to keep their segregated (separate) schools, hospitals, parks, drinking fountains, restaurants, movies, trains, and other areas of daily life. The NAACP had launched drives to register voters in the South. This effort also meant working within the law rather than engaging in mass protest.

Congress of Racial Equality (CORE)

A second group was the Congress of Racial Equality (CORE), organized in 1942. Its strategy was to get people involved in direct action, such as organizing boycotts of segregated places and planning marches to Washington. It tried to bring about change by using nonviolent means. The leaders of CORE hoped to attain their rights in the South by taking the moral high ground. Their tactic was adapted from Mohandas K. Gandhi, who had used peaceful mass action to win independence for India.

Student Nonviolent Coordinating Committee (SNCC)

The newest civil rights group was the Student Nonviolent Coordinating Committee (SNCC, or "Snick" for short), founded in May 1960. It was set up by the students who were staging the lunch-counter sit-ins described in Chapter 1. These young people displayed courage under the abuse heaped on them by segregationists. That brought them support of young white people individually and in groups such as the National Student Association and the National Student Christian Federation. John F. Kennedy, then campaigning for the presidency said, "It is in the American tradition to stand up for one's rights—even if the new way is to sit down."[1]

Southern Christian Leadership Conference (SCLC)

The fourth group—and the main target of Sullivan's lawsuit—was the Southern Christian Leadership Conference (SCLC). It was an outgrowth of the yearlong movement to integrate the city buses in Montgomery, Alabama. That began on December 1, 1955, when Rosa Parks, a forty-two-year-old seamstress, refused to give up her seat to a standing white passenger. She held her ground against the order of the bus driver—even when he threatened to have her arrested. Indeed, two police officers did arrest Parks. They took her first to the police station, then to the city jail. She later recalled, "I simply decided that I would not get up. I was tired . . . and I was not feeling well. I

John F. Kennedy, who was campaigning for the presidency in 1960, supported every citizen's right to stand up for his or her rights.

had felt for a long time that if I was told to get up so a white person could sit, that I would refuse to do so."[2]

Rosa Parks and the Bus Boycott

The simple heartfelt response of Rosa Parks roused her neighbors to action. Jo Ann Robinson, an English professor at Alabama State College, was ready as soon as she heard the news. She was president of the Women's Political Council, an African-American voters group formed in 1946. The group had been hearing how

African-American passengers had been mistreated on city buses for years. Recently, these women had begun to plan to boycott the Montgomery City Lines unless things improved.[3]

The 50,000 African-American citizens, out of the city's population of 120,000, made up the majority of its bus riders. Robinson and her friends printed thousands of leaflets asking "every Negro to stay off the buses Monday," December 5, the day Rosa Parks was scheduled to go to trial.[4] Unless the city officials got the message, readers of the leaflet were told, "The next time it may be you, or your daughter, or mother," who will be arrested. First, the city's African-American church leaders met at the Dexter Avenue Baptist Church, where a twenty-six-year-old minister from Atlanta named Martin Luther King, Jr., had been named pastor the previous year. They decided to announce the boycott at their Sunday services. They organized car pools to pick up people who needed rides to get to their jobs. There would also be taxis standing by. Nothing on this scale had ever been tried. They would meet Monday evening to see whether it had been a success or a failure.

On Monday morning, more than 90 percent of the African-American bus riders stayed away. They walked, caught rides, took mules or wagons to their jobs. Meantime, Rosa Parks was quickly found guilty and

Rosa Parks is shown here being fingerprinted after her arrest in Montgomery, Alabama, on December 1, 1955, for refusing to give up her seat on a bus.

fined fourteen dollars by city court judge John Scott. Hundreds of African-American citizens had gathered outside the courthouse to show their support for Parks. Some of the leaders said they would suggest continuing the boycott at that evening's meeting. Before it ended, they wanted the bus company to offer everyone a chance to sit in vacant seats. The drivers would have to be courteous to African-American passengers, and the company needed to hire some African-American drivers. There was not yet any demand for fully integrated seating.

At the Monday evening meeting, the crowd of about one thousand people was elated. They had been able to empty the city's usually crowded buses. They wanted to keep up the pressure. But so far they had not found a leader. When Dr. King spoke, it was clear that he was the person for the job. He began by praising Rosa Parks for starting the mass protest by her simple action of refusing to give up her seat. Then he said that, like her, all of them were

> tired of being segregated and humiliated, tired of being kicked about by the brutal feet of oppression. We have no alternative but to protest. For many years, we have shown amazing patience. We have sometimes given our white brothers the feeling that we liked the way we were being treated. But we come here tonight to be saved from that patience that makes us patient with anything less than freedom and Justice.[5]

Dr. Martin Luther King's Nonviolent Methods

The kind of protest Dr. King had in mind would be guided by a Christian spirit and the tactics of Mohandas K. Gandhi, who had led the struggle for India's independence (1930–1940), using tactics of nonviolent resistance, such as disobeying unjust laws. King told the audience that he did not want them to hate their white opponents but to love them. They

Dr. Martin Luther King, Jr., was a powerful and persuasive speaker. He and his associate, the Reverend Ralph Abernathy, are shown here at a press conference for the Southern Christian Leadership Conference in Birmingham, Alabama.

must not have anything to do with violence. Yet they needed to go beyond persuasion to use "tools of coercion."[6] It would take determined acts of courage, he said, to change the system of injustice.[7] This speech received a standing ovation.

None of the protesters could have known at that time how long they would have to struggle. They generally expected it to last a week or two. But it would take 381 days—over a year of the boycott—before the courts decided the issue. Until it was over, many of the

African-American leaders of the boycott had either been fired or threatened by their white employers. The city's officials harassed anyone engaged in the protests. They said they would fine black cabdrivers who were charging less than the set fares. They warned drivers in the car pools that they would lose insurance policies and their licenses. The police gave them tickets for supposedly speeding. On January 26, 1956, King himself was arrested for allegedly driving five miles over the 25-mile-per-hour speed limit.

Four days after he was released from jail, King addressed a rally of what had become known as the Montgomery Improvement Association (MIA). During the meeting he was given word that his house had been bombed with dynamite. Fortunately his wife, Coretta, and his baby daughter had not been injured. Before King rushed home, he told the crowd that no one had been hurt and they should go home. He asked them to still love their enemies. He assured them that the movement would go on even without him. Without intending to, Martin Luther King, Jr., had become the personal symbol of the protest movement.

Hatred Toward Dr. King

The young minister was becoming a target for the hatred of the white power structure. He had openly challenged their stereotypes of southern blacks by speaking out. He showed no fear when faced by Ku Klux Klan marches or White Citizens Council mobs. He was an intelligent, well-educated person, with a Ph.D. from Boston University. His outspokenness was at odds with many older black ministers who had not challenged the system. And he was shaking up the society of Montgomery, a city that called itself the "Cradle of the Confederacy." (The Confederate States of America were the eleven southern states that rebelled against the United States in 1861.) Jefferson Davis had been sworn in at the state capitol building on January 7, 1861, as president of the Confederate States. Only two thousand African-American voters were registered in the county, fewer than 7 percent of those eligible. Not a single African American held public office.

Martin Luther King, Jr., was seen by white leaders as an "outside agitator." He recalled that one of them had told him, "Over the years we have had such peaceful and harmonious race relations here. Why have you and your associates come in to destroy this long tradition?"[8] King answered that what had seemed like peace really concealed black servitude. "The tension we see in Montgomery today is the necessary tension that comes when the oppressed rise up and start to move forward toward a permanent, positive peace."[9]

Ironically, the black community was quite divided

when the protests began. The rival organizations argued among themselves. But then an act of white violence, such as the bombing of King's home, brought them back together with renewed unity. The Montgomery boycott struck a chord of nonviolent resistance that was common to CORE, SNCC, and the SCLC. King's electric public speaking ability made him into the spokesman for civil rights groups throughout the South. That prominent role meant that, more than ever, he was becoming a target of white power groups.

Yet King was acutely aware of the lack of "proper facilities and staff," as well as a constant shortage of funds.[10] After a few weeks of the bus boycott, expenses of five thousand dollars a month could no longer be met through local contributions. Donations came from individuals and groups all over the United States and even as far away as Singapore. Appeals for funds brought in the money needed to fight segregation.

Threats and Curtailed Communication

The defenders of the racist system in Montgomery, therefore, pursued twin tactics. They tried to silence Dr. King by making his life in Montgomery as uncomfortable as possible—by threats and legal harassment. They also attempted to cut off his communications with northern supporters. Civil suits for damages against reporters and publishers, such as

Martin Luther King, Jr., was thought of by some white leaders as an "outside agitator."

the *Times*, were designed to isolate King. If they had been successful, they would have limited the civil rights movement to minor local activities.

The African-American protest had begun with very modest demands for changing the seating policy on city buses. The city commissioners would not budge. Indeed, Clyde Sellers, the police commissioner at the time, told a rally of the White Citizens Council on January 6, 1956, that he was joining that racist group. The *Montgomery Advertiser* wrote, "In effect, the Montgomery police force is now an arm of the White Citizens Council."[11] On February 21, city officials indicted more than one hundred of the people, including Martin Luther King, Jr., who had taken part in the boycott. If the protesters did not stop, they could be jailed under a 1921 Alabama law that made it a crime to hinder a business without "just cause or legal excuse."

Each new obstacle raised by their opponents strengthened the resolve of the people who had rallied around King. They kept walking to work, in some cases as far as twelve miles.[12] They turned to Thurgood Marshall, head of the NAACP Legal Defense Fund, for help. Marshall filed a federal lawsuit against the city's segregated bus policy as violating the Fourteenth Amendment. And from the time of the mass indictments, the Montgomery protesters made national news on television and on the front pages of newspapers like *The New York Times*. Martin Luther King, Jr., and other leaders were asked to speak in major northern cities. Outside contributions rose sharply.

Trial Against Boycotting

Meanwhile, on March 19, the state brought Dr. King and his supporters up on the antiboycott charges. During the four days of the trial, defense attorneys presented twenty-eight witnesses. They were ordinary African-American citizens of Montgomery who told of the humiliation they had suffered by using the segregated bus system.

Martha Walker, for example, testified about a time when she was helping her blind husband step down from a bus. "The driver slammed the door and began to drive off. Walker's husband's leg was caught. Although Martha Walker called out, the driver failed to stop, and her husband was dragged some distance before he could free himself. She reported the incident, but the bus company did nothing about it."[13]

Stella Brooks was another defense witness. She told the court that, once, after her husband had paid his fare, the driver told him to get off and board again through the rear door. Mr. Brooks saw that there were no seats in the back of this crowded bus. He "said that he would get off and walk if the driver would return his dime. The driver refused; an argument began; and the driver called the police. The policeman arrived and abused Brooks. He still refused to leave the bus unless his dime was returned, so the policeman shot him. It happened so suddenly that everybody was dazed. Brooks died of his wounds."[14]

Martin Luther King's attorneys had shown through these witnesses that the bus boycott had been provoked by "just cause." Yet Judge Eugene W. Carter at once found Dr. King guilty of breaking the obscure state law. The penalty was $500, plus $500 more for court costs, or 386 days at hard labor. Since King would appeal the verdict, he was released on $1,000 bond and left the courthouse "with a smile." The trial of his associates would be postponed until the appeal was decided.

He later said, "I knew that I was a convicted criminal, but I was proud of my crime. It was the crime of joining my people in a nonviolent protest against injustice." He realized that his opponents "thought they were dealing with a group who could be cajoled or forced to do whatever the white man wanted them to do. They were not aware that they were dealing with Negroes who had been freed from fear."[15]

Still, the city government continued to enforce segregation. It refused to give the African-American population a legal permit to operate its car pools. On April 23, the Supreme Court upheld a ruling that segregated busing in Columbia, South Carolina, was illegal. The Montgomery bus system announced that its drivers would no longer enforce segregated seating either. But W. A. Gayle, the city's mayor, declared he would continue to enforce segregation. Any bus drivers who didn't obey would be arrested.

New Round of Legal Battles

The next round of the legal battle took place before a panel of three federal judges on May 11, 1956. Dr. King said that it was a great relief to be in a federal rather than a state court. Instead of a "prejudiced jury or a biased judge" at the state level, he could now expect "an honest chance of justice before the law."[16] Federal judges had lifetime appointments. They were, as a rule, more independent than elected state judges, who were under pressure by local white segregationists.

The case against segregated busing in Montgomery was presented by Robert Carter of the NAACP legal staff. He argued against the old doctrine of "separate but equal" facilities, which had been rejected by the Supreme Court's 1954 *Brown* v. *Board of Education* decision. Attorneys for the city countered that desegregated buses would lead to racial violence and bloodshed.

Dr. King realized he might get a favorable verdict when one of the judges asked, "Is it fair to command one man to surrender his constitutional rights, if they are his constitutional rights, in order to prevent another man from committing a crime?"[17] About three weeks later, on June 4, the judges announced their two-to-one decision. Alabama's law requiring segregated seating in buses was unconstitutional. The city appealed at once to the Supreme Court, which meant another delay of several months.

Bus Segregation Ends

The bus boycott continued. It took extra money to keep the car pool operating and to have lawyers defend the boycott. On November 13, Martin Luther

Martin Luther King (shown here) was instrumental in ending segregated busing.

King, Jr., faced Judge Carter again. The city of Montgomery had filed a suit to declare the car pool illegal, as undercutting the bus company's exclusive contract. It seemed certain that the judge would rule for the city. During a morning recess, a reporter handed Dr. King a news bulletin. The Supreme Court had affirmed the lower court's order ending segregation on the Montgomery buses. Judge Carter issued his decision against the boycott in the meantime. Another month passed before the Supreme Court issued its decision.

On December 20, federal marshals served the Court's order to the white city officials. The next morning, Martin Luther King was the first passenger to board a city bus on the corner nearest his house. He sat near the front of the bus in a seat formerly reserved for whites. Glenn Smiley, a white minister from Texas, sat in the seat next to him. The national media celebrated this victory of African Americans.

The year a boycott had brought desegregated buses—without separate seats by race—to Montgomery, other southern cities, such as Tallahassee, Florida, followed its example. The boycott had also made King the national spokesman for the civil rights movement. He had warned his supporters not to be overconfident about their victory. "We seek an integration based on mutual respect," he had said. "As we go back to the buses let us be loving enough to turn an enemy into a friend. We must now move from protest to reconciliation."[18]

Dr. King as National Spokesman

Despite these charitable words, King was more than ever hounded by southern segregationists as he expanded his work. On February 13, 1957, nearly one hundred representatives of African-American congregations in ten states met in New Orleans. They called their movement the Southern Christian Leadership Conference (SCLC). They elected King as their president and Ralph D. Abernathy, his close associate, as treasurer. For the next three years, however, this group accomplished little. The defenders of the white-dominated society in the South used violence and legal tactics to resist integration.[19]

King Faces Personal Attack and Arrest

In a typical incident, Dr. King was personally attacked and arrested on September 5, 1958. He had tried to enter the Montgomery courtroom where a trial was to take place of a man who had assaulted the Reverend Ralph D. Abernathy. Two policemen stopped King, then one of them twisted King's arm behind his back. The officers frisked him and took him to the city jail on a charge of "loitering." King said that the policemen "tried to break my arm; they grabbed my collar and tried to choke me, and when they got me to the cell, they kicked me in."[20] At his trial on a reduced charge of resisting an officer, King refused to pay the ten dollar fine plus four dollars court costs. He was marched off to serve two weeks in prison. Clyde Sellers, the police commissioner, realized that this would make the city look bad. He quickly paid the fine for King, and King was released.

King Arrested Again

In February 1960, Dr. King moved his family to Atlanta, where he wanted to set up the SCLC headquarters. He would then direct an ambitious plan to increase registered African-American voters in the South by more than one million. Two weeks after his move, however, two local sheriffs appeared with an arrest warrant. Alabama had charged him with two counts of perjury (lying under oath) for understating his income on his 1956 and 1958 state tax returns. King posted a $2,000 bond. He would return voluntarily to Montgomery to defend himself.

The pending trial was a real threat to King. He could expect to be found guilty of this felony by an all-white jury. He would then face a penalty of as much as ten years in prison. In early March, his friends in New York formed a Committee to Defend Martin Luther King and the Struggle for Freedom in the South, headed by Bayard Rustin. It was this group that ran the ad in *The New York Times* on March 29, which gave rise to Sullivan's libel suit. The money that poured in helped pay for the team of six attorneys who would defend Martin Luther King, Jr.

Dr. King had never won a trial in an Alabama court. This time it began on a hopeful note. On May 25, the fourth day of the trial, the prosecution's chief witness

Dr. Martin Luther King is shown here addressing a meeting at the Mount Zion AME Church in Montgomery, Alabama, in January 1957.

was Lloyd D. Hale, the state's tax auditor. He admitted on cross-examination that he had told King four months before that there was no evidence of fraud in his tax returns.[21] Defense witnesses then testified that the extra income alleged by Alabama was really money for legitimate travel expenses. To the astonishment of the courtroom, the jury returned in less than four hours with a verdict of not guilty. King told the reporters waiting for him outside the courthouse,

> This represents great hope, and it shows that there are hundreds of thousands of white people of good will in the South, even though they may disagree with our views on integration.

Dr. Martin Luther King (seated) and his associate, the Reverend Ralph Abernathy, are shown in a St. Augustine, Florida, jail after their arrest on June 11, 1964, for sitting-in at a segregated restaurant.

Hubert T. Delaney, one of the senior defense lawyers, added that the acquittal was "the most surprising thing in my 34 years as a lawyer."[22]

With his legal problems temporarily over, Dr. King could gather support for the young people who had been staging sit-ins across the South. A new, coordinated strategy of nonviolent action against segregation was being organized. But progress was slow. White officials fought off the peaceful assault by physical and legal means. The libel suits against *The New York Times* and the four ministers affiliated with the SCLC were their latest weapon.

3

The Case for Sullivan

So far, we have looked at the background of the case from a historical perspective. We have seen that it occurred at a crucial moment in the birth of the civil rights movement. The trial in the *Sullivan* case resulted in $2.5 million in damages. It meant that *The New York Times* and the four African-American clergymen would have to pay Sullivan $500,000 apiece. Before appeals of this verdict could be heard, three other Montgomery city commissioners sued the *Times* for libel. Mayor Earl James, commissioner Frank Parks, and former commissioner Clyde Sellers were also seeking half a million dollars apiece in their suits from each of the defendants.[1] Governor John Patterson then filed a million-dollar suit against the *Times*, the four ministers as well as Dr. King, who had not even been listed as a sponsor of the ad.[2]

Neither the *Times* nor the ministers could afford such repeated judgments. If the verdicts were upheld, they would restrict the freedom of reporters writing critical stories about the South. They would also bankrupt civil rights organizations trying to raise funds for the defense of their leaders, whose cars were already being repossessed. Here we turn to the legal issues that were being presented to the United States Supreme Court. They were argued separately from the racial conflict in Montgomery.

Sullivan Raises a Technical Question

As the legal briefs for Sullivan make clear, the question he raised for the higher courts was technical rather than political: Does the Constitution give newspapers the right to defame public officials?[3] Roland Nachman, the head of Sullivan's legal team, answered his own question: "Libelous utterances have no constitutional protection."[4] This argument had the weight of history behind it.

First Amendment Freedom of Speech and the Press

The First Amendment guarantees freedom of speech and of the press. But the members of the First Congress who drafted this addition to the Constitution in 1789 did not think of these as absolute rights. One of the exceptions that America inherited from centuries of English law had to do with libel. A famous English judge named Sir William Blackstone had said that libel of government officials or of private persons was illegal. According to Blackstone, if a citizen "publishes what is improper, mischievous or illegal, he must take the consequences."[5]

The Founding Fathers—the fifty-five members of the convention to draft our Constitution in 1787—had studied *Blackstone's Commentaries on the Laws of England.* They generally accepted his views. Despite the First Amendment, the Federalist majority in Congress enacted the Alien and Sedition Acts in 1798. These laws made it a crime to publish "any false, scandalous writings against the government of the United States."[6] They led to the arrest of many writers, editors, and speakers for "seditious libel." The Republicans were swept back into office in 1801 and repealed the laws. President Thomas Jefferson pardoned all those who had been imprisoned. The Supreme Court had never decided whether or not the Alien and Sedition Acts were constitutional. It would return to that question in 1964 in connection with the *Sullivan* case.

The First Amendment denied Congress the power to lessen freedom of the press. However, it failed to deal with the power of the states in that area. Finally, in 1925, the Supreme Court took care of this omission. In the case of *Gitlow* v. *New York*, a majority of the Justices

As president, Thomas Jefferson pardoned all the people who had been imprisoned under the Alien and Sedition Acts of 1789.

let stand New York's conviction of Benjamin Gitlow for publishing a manifesto of the Socialist party.[7] He was imprisoned for violating the state's law against criminal anarchy, threatening to overthrow the government by illegal means. Yet Justice Edward Sanford's opinion stated that freedom of speech and of the press were "among the fundamental rights and 'liberties' protected by the Due Process Clause of the Fourteenth Amendment from impairment by the states."[8]

What this meant was that the states could prosecute "incitements" under their so-called police power. But the federal courts would see that this power did not prohibit the "utterance or publication of abstract 'doctrine.'"

Justice Oliver Wendell Holmes wrote a famous dissent in the *Gitlow* case. He thought Sanford's distinction made no sense. "It is said that this manifesto was more than a theory, that it was an incitement. Every idea is an incitement. . . .The only difference between the expression of an opinion and an incitement in the narrower sense is the speaker's enthusiasm for the result."[9]

The libel suit in *Sullivan* was not the kind of criminal case represented by Gitlow. No one was being threatened with imprisonment by the state. It seemed to be simply a civil case between two parties, in which money was being sought to repair an injury to someone's reputation. At least that was an essential part of the argument for Sullivan. His lawyers had resisted the appeal of the case by the *Times* to the Supreme Court.

Nachman and his associates argued that the case did not pose a "constitutional question." They quoted President Thomas Jefferson who had condemned any restriction on speech by Congress. He wrote to Abigail Adams in 1804, "While we deny that Congress [has] a right to control the freedom of the press, we have ever asserted the right of the states, and their exclusive right, to do so."[10]

Sullivan's lawyers pointed to the recent record as well. The Supreme Court had declined to review forty-three decisions in libel cases by state and federal courts.

What evidently concerned them was that this time the Justices were reviewing the *Sullivan* case. They might agree with the appeal by the *Times*. So the lawyers painted a grim picture of the consequences of such an outcome. If the Court ruled against Sullivan, they argued, a newspaper might get away with a false story charging the Secretary of the Treasury with embezzling public funds. Or even worse, a state governor could be wrongly accused of poisoning his wife.[11] Such a blizzard of false reports, they said, would turn "the Bill of Rights into a suicide pact.[12]

Supreme Court Overturns Three Separate Libel Verdicts

Nachman was a graduate of Harvard Law School. He had then worked for the Alabama attorney general's office for six years before going into private practice. No doubt, he knew that the forty-three times the Court had not reviewed a libel case were not the whole story. Three times in 1959, the Court had overturned libel verdicts. It might do so again in the *Sullivan* case. The first case was that of a political candidate who was found to have defamed a farmers group during a radio broadcast. The award in state court against radio station WDAY in North Dakota could not stand, the Court said. The station had been obliged under the Federal Communications Act to provide candidates for public office with equal time to air their views. But the federal law said the station then had "no power of censorship over the material broadcast." State libel laws, therefore, could not apply.[13] The *WDAY* decision was the first one in which the Supreme Court set aside a state libel judgment. And its justification was the people's right to obtain political information, which was also an element in the *Sullivan* case.

The other two 1959 cases concerned government workers who had won suits against their superiors for libel. One group of employees claimed they had been libeled in a press release by the acting director of the Office of Rent Stabilization.[14] The second group at the Boston Navy Yard had sued a captain for critical comments he had made about them in an official report.[15] In both decisions the Supreme Court found that federal officials had immunity from libel suits by private parties while performing their duties. The *Sullivan* case would look at the question from a different perspective: Did private individuals have such immunity when they made critical remarks of state or local officials?

The *Times* had been basing its appeal on the First Amendment's stated freedom of the press. Sullivan's lawyers opposed this with reference to the Seventh Amendment. That part of the Bill of Rights guarantees "the right of trial by jury" in civil suits where more than twenty dollars is at stake. Further, it states that ". . . no fact tried by a jury, shall be otherwise reexamined in any Court of the United States, than according to the rules of the common law." In other words, the Alabama jury had spoken, and its word was final.

The jury's verdict should stand, Nachman argued, for three reasons. First, it followed the Alabama law on libel, which was basically the same as that of most other states. Second, it rested on a series of false statements in the advertisement, which *The New York Times* had failed to notice at the time or to retract afterward. Third, its damage award was not excessive in view of the injury to Sullivan's reputation.

Alabama's Libel Law Same as Other States

At first glance, the Alabama law on libel seemed to stack the cards against a defendant. If a government official wanted to sue, he simply had to ask the publisher for a retraction. If the publisher failed to make a public apology, the official could claim libel. The only defense at that stage was proof that the story was completely accurate. Even a minor error in a report robbed the publisher of the so-called absolute defense of truth.[16] Furthermore, if the story merely criticized an agency, such as the Montgomery police, any number of officials could claim they had been injured without being named.

Sullivan had followed these steps. He had not proven that he really suffered any loss because of the

Times ad. But he didn't have to. One of his former employers, the manager of a trucking company, said that he would hesitate to rehire Sullivan if the police misdeeds in the ad were true. Horace White of the P.C. White Truck Line said, "I don' t know whether I'd want to be associated with anybody who would be a party to such things."[17] That was enough to establish a case for damages. Judge Jones was following the state law when he told the jury the libel had been proved per se, that is, in itself. If the jury members believed that the bad actions of the police mentioned in the ad could apply to Sullivan, they had to decide in his favor. All that was left for them to do was to decide on a sum for damages to be paid by the *Times* and by the four clergymen.

Under this state law, there was no limit for the total amount of the damages. There was not even a requirement to prove that the four ministers knew anything about the running of the ad, let alone that they personally signed it. The state court did not have to follow the rule that requires proof "beyond a reasonable doubt." That is the standard for criminal trials, but this was a civil trial. Here guilt could be decided by evidence of greater weight. It would have been possible for Sullivan to sue the *Times* under a rarely used criminal law for libel. But under that law he would have been limited to collecting only five hundred dollars in damages. His victory in the civil suit awarded him a thousand times as much.

Nachman cited one other recent precedent in his brief to the Supreme Court. That was the controversial 1952 decision, *Beauharnais* v. *Illinois*.[18] A bare 5-to-4 majority of the Court had approved a conviction under the state's law against group libel. The law had made it illegal to publish words or pictures portraying the "depravity, criminality, unchastity or lack of virtue of a class of citizens, of any race, color, creed or religion."

Joseph Beauharnais was the president of a group called the White Circle League. He had handed out leaflets on the streets of Chicago that vilified African Americans. These urged city officials to protect whites from the "rapes, knives, guns, and marijuana" of blacks who moved into their neighborhoods. The majority opinion by Justice Felix Frankfurter found nothing wrong with applying individual libel law to groups. It let the two hundred dollar fine against Beauharnais stand. A strong dissent by Justice William O. Douglas said that the tables could be turned. Instead of a white racist, the next defendant might be "a negro [who] will be hailed before a court for denouncing lynch law in heated terms."[19] Justice Douglas turned out to be right in his forecast.

Ironically, the *Beauharnais* decision was now being used by southern whites against four black defendants in Montgomery. Nachman cited it to justify the conduct of the libel suit by Sullivan. He said that the 1952 decision had approved the Illinois judge, "deciding as a matter of law the libelous character of the utterance." It left to the jury "only the question of publications."[20] In other words, the Alabama judge was not exceeding his authority in finding *The New York Times* ad libelous. Nachman further strengthened his argument by showing that Alabama's law was essentially the same as that in a majority of the states.

What the Supreme Court had to decide in 1964 was different from the issue defined by Justice Frankfurter twelve years before. He had not considered the First Amendment central to the questions in *Beauharnais*. He only touched on it at the end of his opinion, saying the First Amendment was irrelevant because prior decisions had put libel outside the area of protected speech. Nachman later admitted that he had been caught off-guard when the *Times* made the free speech and press clause the heart of its case.[21]

Verdict Based on False Statements in Ad

Mr. Nachman seemed to be on firm constitutional ground. In the majority of cases, the Court had left to the states the right to define and punish libel. The only real exception, as mentioned earlier, was that broadcasters were in a special "preferred" position. They

53

could not be prosecuted for following federal law that required them to give equal time to political candidates without censoring what they said. No such reference had been granted to newspapers or to private citizens.

After arguing that Judge Jones had followed the law correctly in the Montgomery trial, Nachman justified the verdict of the jury. Of course, he had no way of knowing what was in the minds of the members of the jury when they acted so quickly to bring in a record judgment for Sullivan. But he said that the jury "was no doubt struck by the amazing lack of concern and contrition exhibited by the *Times'* representatives at the trial."[22] They had retracted the part of the ad that offended Governor Patterson. But their failure to make the same public apology to Sullivan, Nachman said, justified the award of punitive damages.

To show "reckless disregard for the truth" by the *Times*, Nachman listed the false statements in the ad. The third paragraph dealt with student protests in Montgomery. The students did not sing "My Country, 'Tis of Thee," as claimed in the ad, but the "Star-Spangled Banner." Some of them were expelled for the sit-in at the courthouse snack bar, not for the rally on the steps of the state capitol. The police had not "ringed the Alabama State College campus," as the ad said, but they had massed on one side of the campus. Worst of all, there was no official attempt to padlock "their dining hall" in "an attempt to starve them into submission" when students refused to register for a new term.[23]

Then Nachman argued that the sixth paragraph of the ad could also be read to libel Sullivan. This section referred to Dr. King and his persecution by (unnamed) "Southern violators." It could imply that the violators included police. And when the ad said, "they have bombed his home," a reader might infer that also might relate to the Montgomery police. That would implicate Sullivan, though the police had investigated the bombing, admittedly without turning up any suspects. Then, "they have assaulted his person" could also be linked to the police. Nachman argued that the two officers who had arrested King for "loitering" outside the courtroom had not assaulted him, as he had charged. Finally, "they" were said to "have arrested him seven times." But King had been arrested only four times in Alabama: twice by the city (for speeding on January 25, 1956, and for "loitering" on September 3, 1958) and twice by the county sheriff (for violating the state law against boycotts on February 26, 1956, and for falsifying his income tax return on February 29, 1960, a charge on which he was found innocent).

Most of these errors do not seem substantial. What difference does it make what song the students sang? Or on what occasion they were expelled? Or whether Dr.

These students at Alabama State College in Birmingham were demonstrating for integration in February 1960.

King had been arrested four times instead of seven? The only major misstatement was that students had been locked out of their dining hall in an attempt to starve them into submission. For purposes of Alabama law, however, each mistake punctured the defense of the *Times*. When Sullivan had asked for a retraction, the newspaper had owned up to the falsity of only the one sentence about locking the students out of the dining hall.[24] But the *Times*'s lawyers kept insisting that none of the errors had anything to do with actions by Sullivan. Nachman kept hammering on the liability of *The New York Times* for the truth of language in its advertisements. He quoted from the paper's own "Advertising Acceptability Standards" to show that it was supposed to reject "fraudulent or deceptive advertisements" as well as "attacks of a personal character."[25] Yet the ad had slipped through, as D. Vincent Redding, manager of the advertising department had testified. He had approved it because it was signed by "a number of people who were well known and whose motives I had no reason to question."[26] Some of the exaggerations in the ad apparently were added at the last minute. For example, John Murray, who drafted the text, conceded that the names of the four ministers had been included as the "result of a sudden idea by Bayard

Most of the errors in the advertisement in *The New York Times* do not seem substantial enough to warrant concern. Why should it matter whether Martin Luther King (shown here addressing a 1967 rally against the Vietnam War) was arrested four or seven times?

Rustin," who chaired the defense committee for King.[27] The ministers were not asked for permission. Rustin "took their names from a list of ministers in the Southern Christian Leadership Conference."[28]

Some aspects of the charges were not so clear-cut, however. The "Southern violators of the Constitution" were said by the ad to have repressed students representing a "new non-violent brand of freedom fighter" in ten cities. How could this be read as applying to one police commissioner in one city—Montgomery—who had not even been named? A similar question arises about the ad's criticism of the southern violators who "have answered Dr. King's peaceful protests with intimidation and violence." The charge was so general it could be linked to dozens of state and local officials. No specific violator of King's rights had been identified.

Finally, the *Times* had to pay punitive damages for the malice and "reckless disregard of truth" in printing the ad. Yet no witness offered evidence that the paper's advertising managers acted in such a way. Indeed, they could have gone one floor down to the news department to check facts. Their failure to do so may have amounted to carelessness—perhaps negligence—but hardly a malicious intent. The view from Montgomery in the 1960s was quite different from that of a newspaper office in New York.

Damage Award Not Excessive

If Sullivan had asked for a nominal amount of damages, rather than millions of dollars, it is doubtful that his case would have been heard by the Supreme Court. The judgments against the *Times* and the four ministers were the largest ever awarded in Alabama history. Later, Nachman admitted that it had been a mistake to ask for such big sums. He said, "I didn't want to sue for more than a hundred thousand dollars, but the lawyer who'd brought me into the case wanted $1 million dollars, so we compromised on five hundred thousand dollars."[29]

At the time, Sullivan's attorney could not foresee that the other Montgomery commissioners and the governor would sue for the same or even greater amounts. Nor did he know that yet more charges of libel would be filed against the *Times* for a news story published two weeks after the ad for Dr. King. Harrison E. Salisbury's article described the "emotional dynamite of racism" he had found on a visit to Birmingham.[30] Salisbury wrote that the breakdown of a dialogue between whites and blacks was due to "the mob, the police and many branches of the state's apparatus." Eugene ("Bull") Connor, the city's police chief, and other officials sued the *Times* for $3.15 million in damages and Salisbury for an additional $1.5 million.

In his legal argument for the amount due Sullivan,

Nachman cited the $1 million in general damages and $2.5 million in punitive damages recently awarded to a radio commentator by a New York court.[31] John Henry Faulk had sued a magazine called *Red Channels* for falsely linking him to a Communist conspiracy.[32] He had lost his job and could not find other work for a long time. In an editorial, *The New York Times* had praised that verdict for its "healthy effect." The total amount for Faulk was seven times the sum awarded to Sullivan. An appeals court had reduced the original award to Faulk by 90 percent. Still, that was in line with the judgment for Sullivan.

Of course, Sullivan had not lost his job as Faulk had. But Sullivan's lawyer claimed that Sullivan had suffered a great wrong due to the *Times*. In the original trial, Nachman had presented a witness who said that he wouldn't rehire Sullivan for a job with his trucking company if he believed what the ad said. Therefore, the damages could be seen as compensation for problems he might have finding work in the future.

If the Supreme Court followed its long-standing record, the state's judgment against the *Times* could be expected to be upheld. However, there was another side to be heard first.

4

The Case for The New York Times

Herbert Wechsler was picked by *The New York Times* to argue its case appealing the libel verdict of the Montgomery court. He had been an assistant attorney general of the United States from 1944 to 1946. Then he became a professor at Columbia Law School. He had argued a dozen cases before the Supreme Court and was well known as an expert on federalism—the relation of the states to the national government.

To Appeal or Not to Appeal?

Wechsler's first meeting with the executives of the *Times* in the fall of 1962 was discouraging. They were not sure the case would be worth the cost of an appeal.

The precedents (previous decisions in the area) seemed to leave the individual states to make and enforce libel laws. Perhaps, they said, it would be better to accept the damages to Sullivan as one of those rare cases where the *Times* had to admit a mistake.[1] Wechsler managed to persuade the *Times* that an appeal really had a chance, because the Court had recently been expanding the scope of the First Amendment. Orvil Dryfoos, who had just taken over as publisher of the *Times*, agreed that the Court might overturn the Alabama verdict because it hurt the freedom of the press.

The brief, or written argument, for the *Times* had to counter the case made by Sullivan. Nachman had contended that centuries of tradition stood behind the libel law of Alabama. Many precedents decided by the Supreme Court simply put a libelous publication outside the freedoms protected by the First Amendment. Wechsler argued that those cases had dealt only with the libel of private persons.

In contrast, the March 1960 ad had criticized government agencies, such as the Montgomery police rather than private individuals. Could officials like Sullivan (who weren't even named in the ad) use libel law to silence critics of the government?[2] Wechsler admitted that the ad had contained some "inaccurate" statements, such as saying that the "entire student body" at Alabama State College had joined in protests. Yet he pointed out, thirty-two students had been arrested on March 8, 1960, and charged with "disorderly conduct."[3] If their supporters could not speak out, the real injury would be done to American society, not to Sullivan.

In this way, Wechsler's brief turned the tables on Sullivan. The Montgomery police commissioner had, with the consent of the judge and jury, defined the text of the *Times* ad so that it was not speech but libel and, as such, could be punished. Now the *Times* defined Sullivan's action as not really a libel suit but an attempt to deny a vital debate of public issues. Viewed the first way, Sullivan was entitled to collect half a million dollars for the injury to his reputation; in the second version, the entire legal case violated the freedom of the press guaranteed by the First Amendment.

To see the issue in this new light, Wechsler had to go back to the earliest times in United States history. He had to explore what James Madison had meant when he framed the Bill of Rights. And he had to remind the Supreme Court that it had never spoken out against the first major test of the constitutional freedom of speech and press in 1798, when Congress passed the Alien and Sedition Acts.

Alien and Sedition Acts

The surprising opening section of the brief defending *The New York Times* jumps backward nearly two centuries. It invites the Supreme Court to remedy its oversight then by finding the Sedition Act unconstitutional now. Wechsler quotes from the 1798 law, making it a crime "if any person shall write, print, utter or publish . . . any false, scandalous and malicious writing or writings against the government of the United States . . . with intent to defame the said government."[4] In other words, citizens could be convicted for the crime of saying bad things about the federal government and its officers.

Wechsler's point was not that Alabama's libel law was exactly like the Sedition Act passed by Congress so long ago. He argued that, bad as it was, the federal act was less unjust than the state law in three respects. First, as a criminal law, the Sedition Act required the kind of evidence that would prove a defendant guilty "beyond a reasonable doubt." Whereas, the civil law of Alabama needed only to show a defendant guilty by "the preponderance of the evidence," that is, by a balance of condemning facts. Second, the Sedition Act included the Fifth Amendment's protection against double jeopardy, namely, being tried more than once for the same crime. In civil law this safeguard didn't apply. As we saw, several officials in addition to Sullivan sued the *Times* for the same statements in the ad. Third, the federal act set a limit to the fines that could be levied against persons found guilty of violating it. However, the Alabama law allowed virtually "limitless awards of punitive damages," because these sums were meant to teach a lesson to others.[5]

The conclusion was that, if the 1798 Sedition Act could be finally found unconstitutional, then the Alabama law must likewise be rejected. Both laws violated the First Amendment's guarantee of freedom of speech and of the press. Each of them "forbids criticism of the government."[6] They are based on "the theory that top officers, though they are not named in statements attacking the official conduct of their agencies, are presumed" to be injured by what has been said or written about them. They do not even have to prove that they suffered financially in any way to collect damages.

Granted, Wechsler stated, those accused of libeling officials under both the Sedition Act and the Alabama libel law could offer "the defense of truth."[7] As it was recognized in 1798, it would not be easy to have a court accept that defense. John Nicholas, a congressman from Virginia, saw the Sedition Act as "a powerful restriction of the press, with respect to the publication of important truths." Citizens "would be afraid of publishing the truth, as, though true, it might not always be in their power to establish the truth to the satisfaction of a court of justice."[8]

The act had been passed to keep government critics in check. If the critics were accused of seditious libel, they had to defend themselves in courts, which were dominated by biased judges. Wechsler did not need to spell out the parallel to the Alabama situation in the 1960s. It was apparent to the Justices that the cards were stacked against defendants associated with the civil rights movement. Southern judges and juries were also unlikely to accept the "truth" of their statements as a valid defense.

One of the ways in which the opposition fought the Alien and Sedition Acts was to have friendly state lawmakers denounce the laws. James Madison had been instrumental in getting the so-called Virginia Resolutions passed for this purpose in 1798 and 1799. Wechsler's brief quoted the report Madison had issued at that time. He had said, "It is manifestly impossible to punish the intent to bring those who administer the government into disrepute or contempt, without striking at the right of freely discussing public characters and measures."[9] Here was the father of the First Amendment evidently defending the basic right of citizens to criticize government officials.

The lesson of 1798, according to Wechsler, was

twofold. "Neither falsity nor tendency to harm official reputation, nor both in combination, justifies repression of the criticism of official conduct."[10] But this "verdict of history" was ignored by the Alabama courts. They upheld the libel verdict against *The New York Times* (as well as the four ministers) because the ad had contained errors of fact, and it was said to have injured Sullivan's reputation. But the lawsuit had been based on a charge that the ad had accused Sullivan of police brutality. It had thus transformed a law designed for "protecting private reputation to a device for insulating government from attack."[11]

Cantwell v. Connecticut

That sort of libel suit, then, was unconstitutional. The First Amendment was written especially to protect political speech. To show the broadest view of this right, Wechsler quoted from a 1940 decision of the Supreme Court, *Cantwell v. Connecticut.*[12] The case dealt with a Jehovah's Witness who went door-to-door asking residents to listen to a record or to take a pamphlet. Cantwell was convicted of a breach of the peace because these materials attacked the Catholic Church—in a mainly Catholic neighborhood. The unanimous opinion of the Court, written by Justice Owen J. Roberts, admitted that these listeners might well have been offended.

James Madison had been
instrumental in fighting the Alien
and Sedition Acts.

But said the Court, in political or religious beliefs, a
speaker's words were protected by the Constitution.

> The tenets of one man may seem the rankest error to
> his neighbor. To persuade others to his own point of
> view, the pleader, as we know, at times, resorts to exag-
> geration, to vilification of men who have been, or are,
> prominent in church or state, and even to false state-
> ment. But the people of this nation have ordained in
> the light of history, that, in spite of the probability of
> excesses and abuses, these liberties are, in the long
> view, essential to enlightened opinion and right con-
> duct on the part of the citizens of a democracy.[13]

The *Cantwell* opinion extended the freedom of religion in the First Amendment. It was only indirectly

related to the freedom of the press that Wechsler was defending here. The opinion echoed his basic theme: that unfettered debate, including attacks on prominent persons, no matter how exaggerated or even false, was necessary for citizens to take part in the democratic process.

Bridges v. California

Another of the precedents used by Wechsler was also not directly connected to libel law. Like *Cantwell,* it expanded the freedom of expression in the First Amendment. The case was known as *Bridges v. California.*[14] It appealed a contempt citation against Harry Bridges, leader of the West Coast Longshoremen's Union, filed by the Superior Court of Los Angeles County. Bridges had been convicted because he had sent a telegram to the United States Secretary of Labor, criticizing a judge's decision that had gone against his union. The Bridges case was linked by the Court to that of *Times-Mirror Co. v. Superior Court of California. The Los Angeles Times* had also been cited for contempt for its editorials about pending criminal cases, especially one against members of the Teamsters Union charged with assault.

Justice Hugo Black's opinion for the 5-to-4 majority of the Supreme Court reversed both contempt judgments—against Bridges and the newspaper—on the basis of the First Amendment. It took the words of that amendment as absolutely forbidding any law "abridging the freedom of speech, or of the press." As Wechsler now reminded the Court, Justice Black had said that the First Amendment "must be taken as a command of the broadest scope that explicit language, read in the context of a liberty-loving society, will allow."[15]

The implication of Wechsler's use of the *Bridges* decision was that even judges had to withstand sharp criticism. They could restrict the free speech of citizens only in extreme cases, Justice Black had said, when a "clear and present danger" was threatening society. Therefore, Wechsler could argue, Montgomery city officials like Sullivan had to show equally tough hides in the face of their critics.[16]

The brief for the *Times* also had to address the rare cases in which the Court had dealt with libel. In Chapter 4, we touched on two 1959 decisions that exempted federal officials from libel suits by private citizens.[17] These recent rulings let Wechsler argue that the reverse should also be true: Citizens needed a "fair equivalent" of the immunity from libel that had been granted to officials exercising their duties.[18]

James Madison supplied the quote to back this up. "The censorial power is in the people over the Government, and not in the Government over the people." We would say that in our system, it should be the people who supervise or criticize the government. Wechsler asked the Court, in the spirit of the Founding Fathers, to look at the people in their "sovereign capacity"—as the crucial part of our system.[19]

The conclusion that followed was that *any* criticism of governmental conduct was within "the core of constitutional freedom."[20] That is, the logical outcome of the *Times* case was that no one—individual or newspaper—should ever be charged with libel for voicing what was wrong with the government. Such critics were just doing what the First Amendment intended them to do. Indeed, they were doing their civic duty by joining a public debate.

At that point, Wechsler set up a second line of defense. After all, only Justices Hugo Black and William O. Douglas were known to hold the "absolute" view of the First Amendment, that is, to interpret it as allowing no limits on free expression. Presuming the Court might not adopt his libel-free rule for political speech, Wechsler also offered a balancing test. He suggested that the Justices could weigh the "conflicting interests" in cases like this. They could consider two factors: the "official reputation" and the critic's "freedom of political expression."[21] Of course, in his more moderate formula, the First Amendment would be central.

Alabama courts, he said, had "totally rejected" that concern.

Wechsler proposed that there still could be libel suits involving officials like Sullivan. But they would have to meet a higher standard than the current law in Alabama. He said that, for example, such a suit would have "to prove the critic's malice."[22] It would not be enough to show the possible carelessness of the *Times* in accepting an ad without checking all the facts. Instead, the offended party would need to prove that the newspaper staff had set out to do him harm.

The Montgomery judge had told the jury to accept his findings that the ad contained a statement "of and concerning the complainant," and that it had indeed injured Sullivan's reputation.[23] That was going too far. The ad was not directed at Sullivan at all, but at groups such as "the police" or "state authorities" or "southern violators." It had even mentioned just a pronoun, "they," referring to those who had bombed Dr. King's home. The trial judge had been wrong to equate all these general targets with one specific individual.[24]

A major point in the defense for the *Times* at the trial had been to protest that it was a New York newspaper and, as such, should not be sued in Alabama. That now became just an afterthought in Wechsler's argument. The *Times,* he said, had only "a peripheral relationship to Alabama," so it should not have been sued there.[25] The libel judgment would hamper the sending of *Times* reporters to the state. That represented an illegal interference with interstate commerce—a subject the Constitution had left to Congress. In other words, only the federal government could regulate trade among the states.

Finally, the brief for the *Times* asked the Supreme Court to reverse the libel judgment upheld by the Alabama courts. The Court's order should "dismiss the action."[26] Wechsler evidently did not want the case sent back for a retrial under new guidelines. That would be the normal Court procedure. But here it would risk that the Alabama judges would simply arrive at the same result, no matter what instructions they got from the Court. The Justices in Washington did not need to be reminded that southern judges had done nothing so far to enforce school desegregation.

The Case for the Ministers

Wechsler had not directly mentioned the civil rights conflict in his brief. He had merely hinted at it. He said that the state court's decision had the effect of limiting debate at a time when "the tensest issues . . . confront the country."[27] He left the specifics to the attorneys for the four Alabama ministers, who had also appealed their $500,000 libel judgments to the Supreme Court.

The Ministers' Legal Team. This legal team was headed by Harry Wachtel, a Wall Street lawyer. He had befriended Dr. King and set up a foundation to help support the Southern Christian Leadership Conference.[28] Now his brief pointed out how racism had dominated the libel trial. Alabama, he said, had "sweeping racial segregation laws, which reflect the community hostilities and prejudices that were funneled into the courtroom."[29] The brief for Sullivan had said there was no question that there had been a fair trial in Montgomery. Wachtel, however, said that the trial had been held in a "carnival-like atmosphere."[30] Photographers had taken pictures of jurors, undermining their objectivity. African Americans had "intentionally and systematically" been excluded from the jury. The segregated seating in the courtroom had helped to "taint and infect all proceedings."

In short, the setting of the trial made sure that the verdict would go against the *Times* and the African-American ministers. As for the content of their statements, both the First and Fourteenth Amendments should have shielded them from libel charges. Both of these sections of the Constitution "protect criticism and discussion of the political conduct and actions of public officials."[31] Finally, "the enormous sum of $500,000, awarded as punitive damages on a record so thoroughly devoid of crucial evidence, is wholly unconscionable."[32]

Friends of the Court. Several additional briefs backed the arguments for the *Times* and the four ministers. Two of these so-called *amici curiae* (friends of the court) were the *Chicago Tribune* and the *Washington Post.* Both of them argued for the broadest possible press freedom. A third amicus brief was submitted by the American and the New York Civil Liberties unions. Their brief asked the Court to extend the First Amendment to all published criticism of public officials. They said the only restriction that might be justified under the Constitution would be against an "incitement" to violent action.[33]

Then they asked what life for the press might be like under the Alabama libel law. It would mean that "any discussion of public affairs must be either laudatory or couched in such abstract generalities . . . that it would have no interest or impact on the issues of the day."[34] In other words, the state would allow only praise of its government or meaningless statements, never any real criticism. Any comments of substance would certainly be met by costly lawsuits against the publishers.

How would the nine Justices of the Supreme Court react to all these arguments? Would they be able to find a majority to support their decision?

5

The Court Decides

The Supreme Court that considered this case in January 1964 was composed of liberals and conservatives. The liberals were led by Justices Hugo Black and William O. Douglas. They were likely to look for legal reasons to read First Amendment rights in the broadest possible way. That would favor *The New York Times*. Justices John Marshall Harlan II and Tom C. Clark were the most prominent conservatives. They were known to favor a cautious reading of constitutional rights. This approach would suggest following precedents and leaving the Alabama judgment for Sullivan undisturbed.

The guiding spirit of the Court at this time was Chief Justice Earl Warren. Although not known as a leading legal scholar, "the Chief," as he was called by his colleagues, had a clear vision of the reforms required to bring about a system of justice that would include everyone. As the district attorney of Alameda County, California, in the 1930s, Warren had built a reputation as "an effective, tough prosecutor."[1] Since becoming the presiding Justice of the Supreme Court in 1953, he had been able to persuade his colleagues to join him in tackling new issues. The Chief Justice's strong presence gave the Warren Court its distinctive activist air. In its first decade, this Court addressed the rights of African Americans, the general rights of all citizens, and the rights of defendants in criminal trials.

The Rights of African Americans

Warren, himself, had found the grounds in *Brown* v. *Board of Education* that facilitated a unanimous Court to overturn racial segregation in public schools.[2] The Justices had continued to press the cause of school integration in *Cooper* v. *Aaron,* the 9–0 decision that advised Governor Orval Faubus of Arkansas that he could not prevent African-American students from attending Little Rock High School in 1958. No governor, the Court said, has the right to ignore decisions of the Supreme Court.[3]

The General Rights of All Citizens

The Warren Court had also enforced a new rule, "one person, one vote," for equal representation of voters in

The Supreme Court's unanimous 1954 decision in *Brown* v. *Board of Education* overturned legal racial segregation in public schools. It would take many years, however, until fully integrated classrooms, like the one shown here, were common.

state lawmaking districts. That was the landmark 1962 decision of *Baker* v. *Carr*. The majority opinion of Justice William Brennan held that unequal representation would violate the Equal Protection Clause of the Fourteenth Amendment. Voters in districts of below-average population had the right to take their case to federal courts.[4] The two dissenters, Justices Felix Frankfurter and John Marshall Harlan, thought the Court should stay out of such a politically divisive area. (Justice Felix Frankfurter retired soon after this case and was replaced by Arthur J. Goldberg.)

The Rights of Defendants in Criminal Trials

By the time it considered the *Sullivan* case, the Court had also begun to expand basic rights of individuals. In a 1963 unanimous opinion, the Justices established the right of poor defendants in felony cases to be provided with an attorney in state criminal trials. The *Gideon* v. *Wainwright* decision responded to a handwritten appeal by Clarence Earl Gideon from a Florida state prison. Gideon had been arrested for breaking and entering a poolroom. He had no money to hire a lawyer, but the trial court denied his request to appoint a public defender, so he had to defend himself. Justice Black's opinion broke with a twenty-year-old precedent to say that, under the Sixth Amendment, the right to counsel was essential for all defendants facing serious charges.[5]

These cases indicate that the Warren Court might not simply let the libel conviction of *The New York Times* and the four ministers stand. Hundreds of precedents had left state court decisions in place without review by federal courts. In this case, the challenge was to a basic constitutional freedom—the freedom of the press. In addition, it involved an evidently racist atmosphere in the courtroom. From the beginning, it seemed that this would be a controversial decision. Perhaps a Court majority would rule for the *Times*. If it did so on some narrow technical point, it would reverse the

Alabama courts only in this instance without disturbing centuries of precedents.

The first signs of how the Justices felt about this case came on January 6, 1964. That was the day the Court had scheduled oral arguments—a formal hearing when the chief lawyers for the two sides had an hour apiece to present their reasoning. As happens in a controversial case, they were frequently interrupted by questions from the Justices. First, it became clear that the Court wanted the lawyers to go over the facts. What was the exact evidence on which the *Times* had been convicted? Which part of the ad was wrong? How had Sullivan

The majority opinion of Justice William Brennan in *Baker* v. *Carr* enforced the "one person, one vote" rule.

been libeled? Then, some of the Justices challenged each lawyer to justify his legal conclusions.

The attorney for *The New York Times* had the first turn. He immediately staked out the historical basis of his argument. The Alabama decision, he said, "poses hazards for the freedom of the press not confronted since the early days of the Republic."[6] He wanted to turn the Court's attention back nearly two hundred years, when criticism of government officials was a crime. The First Amendment was adopted in 1791 to prevent the muzzling of free expression. Now he saw the Alabama libel law posing the same threat. Therefore, he was offering "the same argument that James Madison made and that Thomas Jefferson made with respect to the validity of the Sedition Act of 1798."[7]

Justice Brennan pursued the point. Was Wechsler claiming that all criticisms of official conduct were protected? The answer was yes. Justice Brennan then asked, "Are there any limits whatever which take it outside the protection of the First Amendment?" Wechsler answered, "I would have to say that within any references that Madison made, I can see no toying with limits or with exclusions. . . . The First Amendment was precisely designed to do away with seditious libel, . . . the punishment for criticism of the government and criticism of officials."[8]

Admittedly, the Court had never reviewed the Sedition Act. The lawyer for the *Times* said, "If James Madison were alive today, so far as anything I can see, anything that he wrote, particularly in the report on the Virginia Resolutions, that the submission that I am making is the submission he would make."[9] How could the Justices rule against the Father of the Bill of Rights?

Justice Potter Stewart pressed further, "Your argument would be the same . . . if *The New York Times* or anybody else had accused this official of taking a bribe?" The reply was, "Certainly." Justice Stewart continued, "or buying his office?" Again, Wechsler said, "Certainly. Of course in the historic period in which Madison was writing, charges of bribery were common, and it was this type of press freedom that he saw in the First Amendment."[10]

At that point, Justice Black underlined how radical the argument for the *Times* was. It held that even lies about public officials in the press had First Amendment protection. What's more, wasn't the *Times* asking the Supreme Court to second-guess a jury's finding "that it [the criticism] is false?"[11] The *Times* was not willing to admit that the Montgomery jury had really ruled on that question, because it "was told" by the judge "that [the ad] was presumably false." Yet the jury had accepted the far-fetched claim of Sullivan's that the

Times ad had linked him to the bombing of Dr. King's home. "It was true that King's home was bombed," Wechsler said. "But it was not true that Sullivan bombed his home, or that we conceived that anyone in the world in his right mind could read this to say that Sullivan bombed his home."[12] The so-called defense of truth under Alabama law could not help the *Times* to fight such preposterous charges.

Still, even a liberal Justice like Arthur Goldberg shied away from the sweeping new press freedom being proposed. Wasn't it true, under that rule, Goldberg asked, that "no public official can sue for libel constitutionally and get a verdict with respect to any type of false or malicious statement made concerning conduct, his official conduct?"[13] Wechsler had to say yes. That

Justice Hugo L. Black, shown here, wrote one of the concurring opinions in the *New York Times* v. *Sullivan* decision.

83

was the way he saw Madison's message across history. Justice Goldberg continued, did that mean "that a citizen would have the right . . . to state falsely, knowingly and maliciously that his Mayor, his Governor, had accepted one million dollars to commit an official act, and . . . the Mayor could not sue for libel?"[14]

Again, Wechsler had to admit, "That is right." But the mayor always had the option of making "a speech answering this charge. And that is what Mayors do. . . ."[15] He then went on to spell out his fallback position. If the Court wouldn't accept the logic of Madison's, he told Goldberg, "You have then a situation here where law should surely attempt an accommodation of conflicting interests, the interests of protecting official reputation, and the interests of freedom of discussion."[16] In other words, Wechsler was offering a compromise. He would accept a narrower libel law than Alabama had, for example, limiting a suit to "proof of damage."[17] His quarrel with the Alabama court was that it had awarded such a big sum to Sullivan without "evidence sufficient to support a finding" that the ad had injured his reputation "in any tangible way."[18]

A Departure From Usual Procedures

Some of the conservative Justices understood that Wechsler was asking the Court to depart from its usual procedure. Instead of examining points of law, he wanted them to second-guess what a judge and jury had found. Justice Harlan asked, "Are we entitled to review the evidence here?" Wechsler insisted that the Court would have to do exactly that to get to the constitutional questions. Without agreeing "that surely there was no evidence to sustain a judgment of this sort," the *Times* was left with the huge damage award, "which is a death penalty for any newspaper if multiplied."[19] That is, there were more libel suits emerging from the Alabama courts. Even a major newspaper such as the *Times* would eventually succumb to such sizable damage awards.

Justice Black challenged Wechsler to say why the Montgomery jury should not have linked Sullivan to the acts blamed on the city police by the ad. Nothing in the ad made it seem as if the police were acting under Sullivan's orders, Wechsler answered. There were too many people involved to blame one city commissioner— "there were 175 policemen" and "a police chief in addition to the commissioner."[20]

The *Beauharnais* Case

"What difference would it make," Justice Black continued, "if he was one of the group, and there are 175 or 200? Do you accept *Beauharnais*?"[21] He was referring to the controversial 1952 decision in which the Court had upheld the Illinois law against libeling any racial or religious group (discussed in Chapter 3).

Wechsler no doubt realized the question was a loaded one. If he said yes, he would offend Justices Black and Douglas, who had strongly dissented in that opinion. If he said no, he might offend Justice Clark, who had been in the majority, as well as other Justices who wanted to follow precedent.

In the first part of his answer, Wechsler said that the current case was different from *Beauharnais*. The earlier decision "had nothing to do with official conduct," which was the heart of the current dispute. In the second part of his reply, Wechsler faced the question directly. If Justice Black wanted to know "whether I think *Beauharnais* should be followed and was correctly decided," he said, "I do not."[22] Wechsler added that the trial judge had been right to rule "when the City of Chicago tried to sue for libel" that the suit should be thrown out, on the grounds that you can't libel a city."[23] It was a forceful but diplomatic answer about a decision that the Court had not followed as precedent.

Then, it was the turn of Sullivan's lawyer to present his case. He began by stating that there had been "overwhelming evidence to support the jury verdict."[24] And jury verdicts in civil cases had the Seventh Amendment to back them up. (In such suits, the amendment provides that, "no fact tried by a jury shall be otherwise reexamined in any Court of the United States, than according to the rules of the common law.") In short, the Supreme Court had no right to review the case. It had always given state courts the last word on libel verdicts. So a review of this case had no basis in the Constitution or in precedents.

The facts, as seen by Sullivan's lawyer, were totally at odds with the statements in the *Times* ad. It was not simply a matter of a few wrong details, like the padlocking of the dining hall to keep Alabama State College students from continuing their protests. That was the only mistake the *Times* had admitted. Justice Goldberg was amazed. "Are you arguing to us," he asked, "that the case went to the jury on the posture that this ad was from beginning to end totally false?"[25] "Yes, sir," Nachman answered. "You are?" Goldberg continued. Then it was Justice Potter Stewart who put Sullivan's lawyer on the spot. "By the 'entire ad,'" he asked, "you mean paragraphs 3 and 6?"[26] Nachman became flustered. He said, "Excuse me. Yes sir, the two paragraphs we complained on, Mr. Justice Stewart."

Could the Supreme Court ever review a state libel judgment? Sullivan's lawyer said only if "this Court finds there is no reasonable basis whatever for it."[27] That would only apply to absurd examples, such as a libel suit "that someone had blond hair."[28]

But surely, Justice Byron White asked, "someone

has to finally decide what libel is that falls outside the protection of the First Amendment?" Even that, Nachman insisted, "is a question of state law." Did he really mean, asked Justice Brennan, that the Court "can't re-examine [it] here as a constitutional question?" At that point, Nachman had to retreat. He couldn't deny the Court's basic responsibility to interpret the Constitution. He explained, so far the Court had never done that in a libel case, but he wasn't saying it could happen under "no circumstances."[29]

Another flat assertion of Nachman's came under fire. He had claimed that the *Times* retracted the ad to avoid a lawsuit by Governor Patterson, but it refused to do so for Sullivan: "It said errors and misstatements, and there was nothing in the ad, your Honor, even suggesting that there was any truth in the ad."[30] Justice Goldberg pointed out that this was an exaggeration. He quoted the letter to the governor. It only apologized if anyone assumed that "the Honorable John Patterson was guilty of grave misconduct"—something the *Times* said it had "never intended to suggest." Goldberg concluded, "That does not go as far as you said."[31]

Justice Goldberg also questioned how Sullivan was identified in an ad that had never named him. For example, he asked, how was he implied by the phrase, "when the entire student body protested to state authorities"

"Your Honor," Nachman answered, "municipal authorities can reasonably be construed by a jury to be state authorities."[32] Even the pronoun "they" could be taken to mean the police, in "the 'they' who arrest for loitering and speeding and the 'they' who arrest for bombing and the 'they' who arrest for assault and murder."[33]

If that were so, Goldberg continued, "what would prevent under your theory of the case any citizen in the South" saying he was libeled by the *Times* ad? Couldn't he claim the ad referred to "southern violators, the 'they' means that I bombed, that I did all these things?" That wasn't possible under Alabama law, Nachman replied, because it "requires a group be sufficiently small so that identification can readily be made."[34] Nachman had to admit that any officer of the local police, however, might have claimed he was libeled by the ad, though a year later, the time had expired for such suits.[35]

Justice White then asked whether Sullivan's claim rested on the charge that the *Times* had deliberately lied. Not quite, answered Nachman. He thought the *Times* defense required convincing "this Court that a newspaper corporation has an absolute immunity from anything it publishes . . . We think that it would have a devastating effect on this nation."[36] He went on to say that no court had "ever made a distinction between libel of public officials and libel of private persons."[37]

The Amount of Damages Questioned

There was a last flurry of questions by the Justices about the size of the damages the trial court had given Sullivan. "If you hadn't asked for $500,000 but for $5 million," asked Justice Brennan, "and the jury had come in with $5 million, I take it on this record you would still be entitled to it?"[38] Nachman again argued that this issue had never come up in prior cases: "The Court has not heretofore gone into the question of the excessiveness or inadequacy of damages." Further, he said, a New York verdict had recently awarded $3.5 million for libel, or seven times Sullivan's award. He conceded that the New York sum had been cut to $350,000 on appeal.[39] But "a smaller award" in Alabama ". . .would have been a slap on the wrist for the *Times*."

The oral arguments were over. The two lawyers had outlined their positions and withstood the barrage of questions. Now it would be up to the Justices to take sides. On the following Friday morning, they met to discuss the case at their weekly conference. At these private meetings they take a vote. The senior Justice of the majority then assigns someone to draft the opinion. Here most of them wanted to dismiss the libel award but on narrow grounds, such as that the ad had not named Sullivan nor injured his reputation.[40]

Chief Justice Warren assigned the case to Justice Brennan. If he had picked Justices Black or Douglas, they could be expected to take the broadest position on press freedom. That would surely split the Court. But Brennan was respected as a scholar and "a balancer of interests."[41] Warren regularly turned to him to find a judicial basis for the desired result. Brennan was known for patiently negotiating with colleagues. He would adjust his opinion until he had a majority supporting it.[42] In the *Sullivan* case, it took Brennan eight drafts—virtually a record—before he had built his majority.[43]

First, Justice Brennan took the fallback position in Wechsler's brief. Libel against public officials would require not just a mistake, such as the *Times* had made in not checking the facts of the ad. It would take a publisher's "malice," or ill will. This was too conservative for Black, Douglas, and Goldberg, who wanted free public discourse with no reservations. These three liberals decided on "concurring opinions." They voted with Brennan but put their broader grounds on the record. Then, Justice Harlan asked Brennan to narrow his definitions so that "a cop, a clerk, or some other minor public official" could file an ordinary libel suit.[44] Harlan and his fellow conservative, Justice Clark, prepared to write dissenting opinions.

Seeking Common Ground

Justice Brennan continued to seek common ground. One account described him as "thin and gray-haired, and his easy smile and bright blue eyes gave him a leprechaun's appearance as he sidled up and threw his arms around his colleagues."[45] He persisted in trying to bring the holdouts into the majority. He was "the most energetic advocate. He cajoled in conference, walked the halls constantly and worked the phones, polling and plotting strategy with his allies."[46]

One of the stumbling blocks had been Justice Brennan's intention to simply overrule the Alabama courts. Otherwise, they might keep ruling against *The New York Times* and the ministers who supported Dr. King. The final draft, however, offered to send the case back to the Alabama supreme court "for further proceedings not inconsistent with this opinion." This move by Brennan persuaded Justice Stewart, then Harlan and Clark to come aboard.[47] It had taken just two months—a relatively short time—to decide such a complex case.

At 10 A.M., on Monday, March 9, 1964, the Chief Justice signaled Justice Brennan to proceed. Brennan said, "I have for announcement the opinion and judgment of the Court in number 39, *New York Times Co. v. L.B. Sullivan.*"[48] He read the lengthy decision, as reporters made notes for the following day's front-page stories. There were four main sections: (1) a reversal of the Alabama libel judgment against the *Times* and the four ministers, (2) a historical look back at the Sedition Act of 1798, (3) a reexamination of the First Amendment, as it applied to the role of public debate, and (4) a new standard of laws against libel of public officials.

Alabama Libel Judgment Reversed

All nine Justices agreed that the Alabama courts had been wrong in finding that the defendants were guilty of libel. The advertisement was protected by the First Amendment's guarantee of free expression. Justices Goldberg, Black, and Douglas were ready to support this as an absolute right. They explained this in separate concurring opinions. The other six Justices would offer the protection to the media unless a plaintiff could show that statements against him had been made with "actual malice."

Sullivan could not receive damages for two reasons. First, said Justice Brennan, "injury to official reputation" could not be an excuse for repressing someone's speech. Criticism of a person's "official conduct does not lose its constitutional protection merely because it is effective criticism and hence diminishes" his reputation.[49] Second, there was not sufficient evidence in the ad's text for the jury to conclude the text even referred to Sullivan. The six witnesses who testified otherwise had not "suggested any basis for the belief that the respondent [Sullivan] himself was attacked in the advertisement beyond the bare fact that he was in overall charge of the police department and thus bore official responsibility for police conduct."[50]

The Sedition Act of 1798 Is Reviewed

Justice Brennan accepted Wechsler's challenge to finally condemn the Sedition Act. After 166 years, he noted, it was time to acknowledge "the attack upon its validity has carried the day in the court of history."[51] This was crucial because it highlighted the central place of the First Amendment in permitting criticism of government and public officials. It also followed that the Alabama libel law offered an even greater threat to free speech. It imposed a hundred times greater penalties than the Sedition Act and lacked any safeguard against double jeopardy. "Whether or not a newspaper can survive a succession of such judgments, the pall of fear and timidity imposed upon those who would give voice to public criticism is an atmosphere in which First Amendment freedoms cannot survive."[52]

Reexamining the First Amendment

Justice Brennan had to contend with the precedents cited by Sullivan's lawyer. In the past, the Court had set

All nine Justices of the Supreme Court agreed that the Alabama courts had been wrong in finding that *The New York Times* was guilty of libel.

libelous words apart from constitutionally protected speech. It was time to reject such outworn labels, said Justice Brennan. "Libel can claim no [special] immunity from constitutional limitations. It must be measured by standards that satisfy the First Amendment."[53] Democracy required speech with the least possible restriction. In a memorable sentence, Brennan said this case had to be viewed

> against the background of a profound national commitment to the principle that debate on public issues should be uninhibited, robust, and wide-open, and that it may well include vehement, caustic, and sometimes unpleasantly sharp attacks on government and public officials.[54]

A New Standard of Libel Laws

Alabama libel law was wrong not only in shielding state officials from criticism but also in insisting on the "defense of truth," Justice Brennan said. "Erroneous statement is inevitable in free debate." Therefore, even false statements "need to be protected if the freedoms of expression are to have the 'breathing space' that they need . . . to survive."[55] State laws requiring "the critic of official conduct to guarantee the truth of all his factual assertions"—or to face huge libel awards—lead to "self-censorship."[56] Even if critics think their attack on an official is true, they would hesitate to speak out "because of doubt whether it can be proved in court or fear of the expense of having to do so."

Such state libel laws could not continue. The new standard of the Court was that "a public official" cannot recover "damages for a defamatory falsehood relating to his official conduct unless he proves that the statement was made with actual malice—that is, with knowledge that it was false or with reckless disregard of whether it was false or not."[57]

Any further state action on this case would have to take place within these new 1964 guidelines.

96

6

The Impact of the *Times* Decision

The next day's edition of *The New York Times* had a front-page story about the decision. "The case could have an immediate effect on press coverage of race relations in the South," it said.[1] The *Times* had been facing a total of $5 million in libel suits from Alabama. The Columbia Broadcasting System was being sued for $1.5 million. *Times* publisher Arthur O. Sulzberger commented, "We are of course delighted with the decision of the Supreme Court. . . . The opinion of the Court makes freedom of the press more secure than ever before."[2]

A Victory for *The New York Times*

An editorial in the March 10 issue called the *Times* decision "a victory of the first import in the . . . struggle for the right of a free press." It was a vital function of newspapers "to encourage the free give-and-take of ideas and, above all, to be free to express criticism of public officials and public policies. This is all part of the lifeblood of a democracy."[3]

The issue also had news of the four African-American ministers who had been targets of the same suit. It quoted their attorney, who said Alabama had seized about seventy-five hundred dollars of their property to pay damages to Sullivan. The cars of the Reverends Shuttlesworth, Lowery, and Abernathy had already been sold by the state, as had a piece of Abernathy's land.[4] They could now expect to retrieve their money.

There were no quotes from the losing side. But George Wallace, the new governor of Alabama, did not hide his disapproval. He said he was "not surprised at anything the Supreme Court does."[5]

Response From Legal Scholars

The response from legal scholars was mostly positive. Harry Kalven, Jr., an authority on the First Amendment said that, in *Sullivan*, the Supreme Court had taken "very high ground indeed."[6] It had checked the "human inclination to condemn bad speakers and forget the broader commitment and need of a democratic society for a vigorous policy of open debate." In other words, the decision had warned Americans not to be shortsighted about their interests. Instead, they had to realize that there was a price to be paid for self-government.

Kalven quoted Alexander Meiklejohn, a philosopher, who had been a lifelong advocate of maximum freedom of expression under the First Amendment. Meiklejohn said that *The New York Times* decision was "an occasion for dancing in the streets."[7] Both Kalven and Meiklejohn gave special praise to one passage by Justice Brennan. He had written that "the citizen-critic of government" should have the same rights that "a public official [has] when he is sued for libel by a private citizen. For the ordinary citizen has "as much [a] duty to criticize as it is the official's duty to administer."[8]

Concurring Opinion

Justice Black had written a concurring opinion saying that the majority decision had not gone far enough. It should not have set up "actual malice" as a remaining check on critics of official conduct. "Malice, even as defined by this Court," said Black, "is an elusive, abstract concept, hard to prove and hard to disprove."[9] He would have preferred to reverse the libel judgment "exclusively on the ground that the *Times* and the individual defendants had an absolute, unconditional right to publish . . . their criticisms of the Montgomery agencies and officials." Yet after the *Sullivan* decision, Black sent Brennan a note. It said, "You know, of course, that despite my position and what I wrote, I think that the *Times* case is bound to be a very long step toward preserving the right to communicate ideas."[10] The cheers for the decision were not unanimous. It received a mixed review from one legal scholar. He said the "legal world was stunned" by the decision. But he also thought the *Times* rule "may become a cornerstone of our First Amendment freedoms."[11]

Another law professor complained that here the Supreme Court was "fashioning a nuclear blunderbuss with which to swat a gnat."[12] He was especially critical of the Court for extending protection to false statements, which do not "add much to the marketplace of ideas." He also feared that the *Times* decision would give the green light to verbal assaults in the media. That could lead the press to invade the privacy of citizens. Ordinary people might actually hesitate to comment on public concerns, because they could then be libeled without any recourse.

Critics of the Decision Speak

What bothered the critics? Mainly three things: First, that the Court could have ruled against Sullivan without overturning centuries of libel law. Second, that it was not clear from the decision how large the circle of

The *New York Times* v. *Sullivan* decision got a mixed review from one legal scholar, much as the integration shown at this lunch counter received mixed reviews.

"public officials" was who could be open to all except malicious attacks in the media. And third, that the decision had not clearly defined "actual malice" or "reckless disregard of truth"—the grounds on which even officials could continue to sue for libel.

Overturning Libel Law Unnecessary

For better or worse, all the Justices had joined in ruling for *The New York Times* on broad rather than narrow grounds. As Geoffrey Stone concluded almost thirty years later, the decision "revolutionized the law of

101

libel."[13] The new approach was bound to cause problems. But additional cases would allow the Court to fill in the details. Stone explained that the case came at a critical time. "New York *Times* was, in short, a product of the civil rights movement of the 1950s and 1960s." The Justices realized that "the advertisement was designed to dampen the drive for civil rights. After all, if this Alabama jury's massive damage award could be sustained on the basis of such minor inaccuracies, then no person or institution would be free to challenge racial segregation in the South."[14] The decision was "thus not only a triumph for free expression, it was a triumph for civil rights and racial equality as well."[15]

Justice Brennan had merely hinted at the importance of public debate on this issue in particular. Indeed, without the *Times* decision the civil rights movement might have taken much longer to reach its goals. The subsequent years brought marches and protests to secure voting rights, full desegregation of eating places, hotels and other facilities, and the passage of federal civil rights laws.

One historian noted, "Nobody seemed more effective than Martin Luther King, Jr., in mobilizing national public opinion via television."[16] If the Alabama judgment against CBS as well as *The New York Times* had not been overturned, Dr. King's message might not have reached the public. His ability to recruit volunteers and raise funds would have been jeopardized. Also Congress and the president would not have responded as quickly.

Every Public Official Subject to Criticism

Of course, the immediate effect of the *Times* decision was to enhance the freedom of the media greatly. At least public officials—from the city to the national level—now seemed fair game for critical articles, editorials, even advertisements. Would the Supreme Court limit this rule to comments made about officials when related only to their public acts? And just in civil libel cases, where money was sought to compensate for "injuries"?

Justice Brennan had the opportunity to expand his *Times* opinion eight months later. Orleans Parish district attorney, Jim Garrison, had accused eight district judges of hampering his investigations into prostitution and other vice crimes. At a press conference, he had said the judges were lazy and inefficient, always taking vacations. They had refused to approve funds for Garrison's expenses. He said that raised "interesting questions about the racketeer influence on our eight vacation-minded judges."[17] (Racketeers are people who operate illegal, dishonest businesses.) Garrison was convicted of libel.

Justice Brennan's opinion on November 24, 1964, overturned Garrison's conviction for criminal libel. He said that the *Times* rule applied to criminal as well as civil libel. And it made no difference that the charges had attacked the judges' private character.

> Any criticism of the manner in which a public official performs his duties will tend to affect his private as well as his public reputation. . . . The public-official rule protects the paramount public interest in a free flow of information to the people concerning public officials, their servants. To this end, anything which might touch on an officials fitness for office is relevant. Few personal attributes are more germane to fitness for office than dishonesty, malfeasance, or improper motivation, even though these characteristics may also affect the officials private character.[18]

The new public-official rule affected criminal libel laws in all fifty states.[19] The rule stated that, in general, most people occupying public office had to weather what critics said about them in print or on the air. It would be extremely difficult for such people to show that the words had been said with actual malice, that is, that a reporter or broadcaster was out to get them. How could you tell what was in a critic's mind unless telltale notes were left behind?

Still, the Court under Chief Justice Warren could not always agree on how carefully publishers had to check their facts. In two 1967 civil libel cases, the Justices split 5-to-4. The outcome was determined by which side Warren was on. In the first case, General Edwin A. Walker had been awarded $500,000 in compensatory and $300,000 in punitive damages by a jury. Walker had objected to an Associated Press story that blamed him personally for taking charge of a violent crowd blocking James Meredith's admission to the University of Mississippi. All the Justices wanted to overturn that libel judgment. But the five in the majority said that in a retrial the actual malice test should apply. The minority of four said that "public figures" like Walker, unlike "public officials," could sue, using a lower standard. (Public officials hold government office. Public figures have not been specifically defined in courts, but they are generally people in the public eye due to their actions.) All they needed to prove was that the media had made "an extreme departure from the standards of investigation and reporting" used "ordinarily . . . by responsible publishers."[20] That sounded more like proving negligence than the malice of the *Times* opinion.

Chief Justice Warren helped make another 5-to-4 majority in a companion case to Walker's. This one concerned Wally Butts, football coach of the University of Georgia. Butts had won a $460,000 judgment against *The Saturday Evening Post* for an article accusing him of rigging a game. He was alleged to have called Alabama coach Paul Bryant to tell him play secrets. Here the majority sided with Butts. The difference with Walker's case, Justice Harlan said, was that this story was not

Dr. Martin Luther King (shown here with his wife and children) received the Nobel Peace Prize in 1964 for leading the African-American struggle for equality through nonviolent ways.

"hot news." The weekly magazine should have taken the time to check its facts.[21]

What was significant about these two cases is that neither Walker nor Butts were public officials. But even as public figures, the *Times* rule was going to apply to them. It was also clear from the narrow decisions that the Court tended to split on how broad that rule ought to be. The maximum degree of press freedom was being granted when "hot" issues engaged the public. But the Justices were having second thoughts about letting the media attack prominent persons without restraint.

Definitions Unclear

What was a working definition of the "knowing or reckless falsehood" that could open any publisher to the charge of malice? The Court had a chance to answer that question in April 1968. It was deciding a Louisiana case, which had begun in 1962, two years before the *Times* rule had been announced. United States Senate candidate Phil A. St. Amant used a television broadcast to read a labor official's sworn statement. It accused the president of a Teamsters Union local of bribing Deputy Sheriff Herman Thompson. Thompson sued and won $5,000 in damages for libel.

The state appeals court reviewed the case in 1966, using the *Times* rule. It said that Thompson was a public official and therefore should have first proved the attack on him was based on reckless disregard for truth. That reversed the trial court.[22] In 1967, the Louisiana supreme court reversed the appeals court. It found that St. Amant had indeed used a reckless falsehood in the broadcast. He would have to pay damages.[23] Now the United States Supreme Court, by an 8-to-1 vote, said that was wrong. The original judgment was not valid.

The record showed that St. Amant had falsely accused Thompson and that he should have checked the union official's statement first. But there was no evidence that he had made the accusation without believing it was true. Negligence wasn't enough to uphold libel against a public official. Justice Byron White's opinion said, "There must be sufficient evidence to permit the conclusion that the defendant in fact entertained serious doubts as to the truth of his publication. Publishing with such doubts shows reckless disregard for truth and demonstrates actual malice."[24]

Justice White concluded that there was no single way to define reckless falsehood. He said that "inevitably its outer limits will be worked out by case-to-case adjudication."[25] That meant judges—when necessary the Justices of the Supreme Court—would have to decide the standard in each case. Juries would have the responsibility to determine whether the publication was indeed made in good faith.

Dissenting Opinion

Justice Abe Fortas dissented in this case. He said that a public official should be able to sue if he were "needlessly, heedlessly, falsely accused of crime."[26] Fortas thought the majority had gone too far. "The First Amendment does not require that we license shotgun attacks on public officials in virtually unlimited open season," he said. "The occupation of public officeholder does not forfeit one's membership in the human race."[27]

In 1969, Chief Justice Warren retired. President

Nixon appointed Warren Burger as his replacement, as well as three other Justices later. As a whole, the Court became more conservative. When it came to libel cases, it kept the basic ruling of *New York Times* v. *Sullivan*. But unlike the Warren Court, it tended to side more with the plaintiff, the party bringing the suit for libel, than the publisher.

Gertz v. Robert Welch, Inc.

In the 1974 case, *Gertz* v. *Robert Welch, Inc.*, the Court majority, for the first time, named a prominent person as a private individual, rather than a public figure, in a libel suit. Elmer Gertz was a well-known Chicago attorney who handled a civil suit for a family whose teenage son had been killed by a police officer.

The John Birch Society's magazine, *American Opinion*, accused Gertz of being part of a Communist conspiracy, simply because he accused local police of wrongful acts. The article called him a "Leninist," a "Marxist" and a "Communist-fronter." A federal district court ruled for Robert Welch, the magazine's publisher, under the *Times* rule.

Justice Lewis F. Powell's opinion balanced the values of "uninhibited, robust and wide-open debate" (from the *Times* decision) with the need to compensate persons "for the harm inflicted upon them by defamatory falsehood."[28] Public figures and officials would have to prove "actual malice" to win a libel judgment. They could fight lies about them because they had access to the media to set the record straight. But private persons lacked such "effective opportunities for rebuttal."

A second difference was that public figures had chosen to "occupy positions of . . . power and influence."[29] We would say they knew that to be in the kitchen, they would have to stand the heat. The rest of us, however, are not prepared for a media attack. But we still want to protect our good name. A private individual, therefore, "has a more compelling call on the courts for redress of injury."[30] Therefore, the fifty states should set up "appropriate standards for" libel suits by private persons against "defamatory falsehood" injuring their reputation.[31]

That is, they needed to have libel laws based on proving a publisher's negligence. Here, the Supreme Court was stepping back from deciding libel rules case by case. It was telling states they could develop their own standards. However, they would all have to compensate victims of libel only for an actual injury. And if the courts awarded punitive damages, they would be limited by "the gentle rule that they not be excessive." In general, courts also had to refrain from punishing "unpopular opinion rather than to compensate individuals for injury."[32]

Four of the Justices dissented in the *Gertz* case.

Justice White objected to the fact that the majority had set up nationwide rules for libel law. "From the very founding of the Nation," he said, "the law of defamation and the right of the ordinary citizen to recover for false publication injurious to his reputation have been almost exclusively the business of state courts and legislatures."[33] Under the old law, a citizen had to prove only that a "false publication would subject him to hatred, contempt or ridicule."[34] That was enough to claim "damages"—that is, money to make good the injury. Now, White said, the Court had "federalized major aspects of libel law"[35] and made the old law appear unconstitutional. These were "radical changes in the law and severe invasions of the prerogatives of the States."[36] Chief Justice Burger agreed with White that it was wrong to make such a sharp departure from existing law.

Justice Douglas disagreed with the majority because he wanted the First Amendment to be read as broadly as possible, without any compromises. Justice Brennan said that the *Gertz* opinion gave too much leeway to the states in setting limits to free and robust debate. That would require applying the *Times* rule to libel against public as well as private persons. He considered the "reckless disregard of truth" to be the best definition for libel "in matters of public concern." It was also "a legal fiction," he said, that public figures had access to answer charges against them in the media, whereas private persons kept their lives "carefully shrouded from public view."[37] Minor officials or those who had left office were often ignored when they protested attacks. Even if the publisher printed a retraction of a false story, it "rarely receives the prominence of the original story."[38]

The *Gertz* decision marked a decade since *New York Times* v. *Sullivan* had been announced. It showed that the hopes and fears aroused in 1964 had been exaggerated. Many of the basic rules for libel suits were still being followed, at least when ordinary people were the plaintiffs. Even suits by officials and other prominent plaintiffs were still being filed in large numbers.

The Warren Court had united behind the *Times* opinion, applying First Amendment rights to libel suits in the fifty states. It had set a high standard—actual malice—that public officials had to satisfy before suing a publisher. It had later expanded that protection of the press even when stories were published about public figures. Now the *Gertz* opinion also brought libel suits by private persons under the First Amendment. However, they only had to prove that a publisher had been at fault, for example, by neglecting to check facts in stories that injured them. Suits also could not be based on statements of opinion, as opposed to facts.

The Justices had been unanimous in 1964. Now they often split, with some major cases decided 5 to 4. They had expected the *Times* ruling to bring clarity nationwide to the various state laws on libel. The critics of the decision feared that public officials "would be at the mercy of irresponsible journalism."[39]

Neither outcome seems to have happened. Even thirty-five years later, the basic terms—*malice, public official, public figure*—are still the subject of lawsuits. And there are more libel suits than ever, about 718 between 1973 and 1983. The defendants win the great majority of cases. But even a major publisher or television network has to bear the rising costs of a lawsuit. It took Oprah Winfrey more than a million dollars to defend herself in a six-week libel trial in Amarillo, Texas. She was being sued under the state's "veggie libel" law for saying on her talk-show that she wouldn't eat hamburgers anymore. Her lead lawyer echoed the *Times* ruling when he said, "This case is about the First Amendment. It's about robust debate and it's about the unfettered interchange of ideas."[40] The federal jury ruled that Winfrey was not liable for the fall in beef prices. The public figures who have sued for libel must also have enough money to go to court for prolonged trials and appeals. During the 1980s they included Israeli General Ariel Sharon's suing *Time* magazine, the

113

Reverend Jerry Falwell v. *Penthouse* magazine, and *General William Westmoreland* v. *Columbia Broadcasting System*. The *Times* rule affected the outcome of all these trials. General Sharon won a moral victory when the jury said a *Time* magazine reporter had been negligent, though it found no malice to justify damages. The Reverend Falwell's suit was dismissed, because he did not dispute the accuracy of an interview, just its appearance in *Penthouse*. And the *Westmoreland* suit was settled by CBS just before the trial.[41]

Has the *Times* decision made publishers and broadcasters freer in their attacks on public figures? The general practice seems to be to check all facts carefully before a reporter files a story. If falsehoods come to light, retractions are routinely issued, though they may not fully satisfy the subject of the story. The media generally take care to maintain their credibility, not just to avoid libel suits. It could be argued that the press is, more than ever, a counterweight to governmental power. *New York Times* v. *Sullivan* has become an essential way to update the First Amendment for our increasingly complex society. The courts have been fine-tuning its original findings, but the core of the opinion remains: to assure "that debate on public issues should be uninhibited, robust, and wide-open."

Chapter Notes

Chapter 1. A Clash in Montgomery

1. Harvard Sitkoff, *The Struggle for Black Equality, 1954–1992* (New York: Hill and Wang, 1993), p. 36.

2. Ibid., p. 62.

3. Adam Fairclough, *To Redeem the Soul of America: The Southern Christian Leadership Conference and Martin Luther King, Jr.* (Athens: University of Georgia Press, 1987), p. 61.

4. Rodney A. Smolla, *Suing the Press* (New York: Oxford University Press, 1986), p. 32.

5. Ibid.

6. Anthony Lewis, "Annals of Law: the Sullivan Case," *The New Yorker*, November 5, 1984, p. 54.

7. *New York Times* v. *Sullivan*, 376 U.S. 254, "Briefs," II, pp. 579–580, October 1962.

8. Ibid., p. 43.

9. Ibid., pp. 847–864.

10. Ibid., p. 943, citing the *Alabama Journal* and *Montgomery Advertiser*, November 1, 1960.

11. Ibid., p. 946, citing "Will They Purge Themselves," *Montgomery Advertiser*, April 7, 1960.

12. Ibid., p. 945.

13. Anthony Lewis, *Make No Law: The Sullivan Case and the First Amendment* (New York: Random House, 1991), p. 29.

14. *New York Times* v. *Sullivan*, 144 So. 2d 50.

15. Ibid., p. 37.

16. 376 U.S. 254, "Briefs," III, p. 2092.

17. Ibid., p. 2079.

18. Clifton Lawhorne, *The Supreme Court and Libel* (Carbondale, Ill.: Southern Illinois University Press, 1981), p. 33.

Chapter 2. Civil Rights at a Crossroads

1. Harvard Sitkoff, *The Struggle for Black Equality, 1954–1992* (New York: Hill and Wang, 1993), p. 81.

2. David Garrow, *Bearing the Cross: Martin Luther King and the Southern Christian Leadership Conference* (New York: William Morrow, 1986), p. 12.

3. David Garrow, ed., *The Montgomery Bus Boycott and the Women Who Started It: The Memoir of Jo Ann Gibson Robinson* (Knoxville, Tenn.: University of Tennessee Press), 1987, p. 20.

4. Ibid., p. 46.

5. Martin Luther King, Jr., *Stride Toward Freedom* (New York: Ballantine Books), 1958, p. 50.

6. Garrow, *Bearing the Cross*, p. 24.

7. Ibid.

8. King, Jr., p. 31.

9. Ibid., p. 32.

10. Ibid., pp. 63–64.

11. Cited in Garrow, *Bearing the Cross*, p. 52.

12. King, p. 44.

13. Ibid., p. 120.

14. Ibid.

15. Ibid., p. 122.

16. Ibid., p. 123.

17. Ibid., p. 124.

18. Ibid., pp. 137–138.

19. Sitkoff, p. 57.

20. Cited in Garrow, *Bearing the Cross*, p. 108.

21. Taylor Branch, *Parting the Waters: America in the King Years, 1954–63* (New York: Simon & Schuster, 1988), p. 308.

22. Ibid., p. 309.

Chapter 3. The Case for Sullivan

1. *New York Times* v. *Sullivan*, 376 U.S. 254, "Briefs II" October 1962, p. 960.

2. Taylor Branch, *Parting the Waters: America in the King Years: 1954–63* (New York: Simon & Schuster, 1988), p. 312.

3. *New York Times* v. *Sullivan,* "Brief for Respondent," October 1963, p. 28.

4. Ibid., p. 29.

5. William Blackstone, *Commentaries,* I:152, 1766, cited in David O'Brien, *Constitutional Law and Politics: Civil Rights and Liberties* (New York: W. W. Norton & Co., 1991), p. 338.

6. O'Brien, p. 342.

7. 268 U.S. 652, 1925.

8. Ibid.

9. Ibid.

10. 376 U.S. 254, Brief for Respondent, p. 31.

11. Ibid., p. 34.

12. Citing dissent of Robert Jackson in *Terminiello* v. *Chicago,* 337 U.S. 1, 1949.

13. *Farmers Educational & Cooperative Union of America, North Dakota Division* v. *WDAY, Inc.,* 360 U.S. 525, 1959.

14. *Barr* v. *Matteo,* 360 U.S. 564, 1959.

15. *Howard* v. *Lyons,* 360 U.S. 593, 1959.

16. 376 U.S. 254, "Brief for Respondent," p. 23.

17. 376 U.S. 254, "Briefs," II, p. 664.

18. 343 U.S. 250, 1952.

19. Ibid.

20. 376 U.S. 254, "Brief for Respondent," p. 39.

21. Anthony Lewis, *Make No Law: The Sullivan Case and the First Amendment* (New York: Random House, 1991), p. 161.

22. 376 U.S. 254, "Brief for Respondent," p. 45.

23. 376 U.S. 254, "Briefs," I:2.

24. Ibid., II:590: *See also* "Brief for Respondent," p. 11.

25. 376 U.S. 254, "Briefs," II:598.

26. Ibid., p. 963.

27. Ibid., p. 961.

28. Ibid., p. 963.

29. Lewis, p. 161.

30. "Fear and Hatred Grip Birmingham," *The New York Times*, April 12, 1960, p. 1.

31. 376 U.S. 254, "Brief for Respondent," p. 41.

32. *Faulk* v. *Aware, Inc.*, 231 N.Y. Supp. 2d 270 (1962).

Chapter 4. The Case for *The New York Times*

1. Anthony Lewis, *Make No Law: The Sullivan Case and the First Amendment* (New York: Random House, 1991), p. 107.

2. 376 U.S. 254, "Brief for Petitioner," p. 30.

3. Ibid. p. 8.

4. Ibid., p. 46.

5. Ibid., pp. 31, 49.

6. Ibid., p .30.

7. Ibid., p. 46.

8. Ibid.

9. Ibid., p. 45.

10. Ibid., p. 30.

11. Ibid., p. 50.

12. 310 U.S. 296, 1940.

13. Ibid.

14. 314 U.S. 252, 1941.

15. 314 U.S. 263, 1941.

16. 376 U.S. 254, "Brief for Petitioner," p. 43.

17. *Barr* v. *Matteo*, 360 U.S. 564, 1959; *Howard* v. *Lyons*, 360 U.S. 593, 1959.

18. 376 U.S. 254, "Brief for Petitioner," p. 56.

19. Ibid.

20. Ibid., p. 51.

21. Ibid., p. 52.

22. Ibid., p. 54.

23. Ibid., p. 59.

24. Ibid., pp. 60–61.

25. Ibid., p. 87.

26. Ibid., p. 90.

27. Ibid., p. 68.

28. Taylor Branch, *Parting the Waters: America in the King Years: 1954–63* (New York: Simon & Schuster, 1988), p. 582.

29. 376 U.S. 254, "Brief for Petitioner," p. 12.

30. Ibid., p. 13.

31. Ibid., p. 30.

32. Ibid., p. 35.

33. 376 U.S. 254, "Brief of the ACLU and NYCLU as *Amici Curiae*," p. 17.

34. Ibid., p. 20.

Chapter 5. The Court Decides

1. Melvin Urofsky, "Earl Warren," in Kermit Hall, ed., *The Oxford Companion to the Supreme Court of the United States* (New York: Oxford University Press, 1992), p. 913.

2. 347 U.S. 483, (1954).

3. 358 U.S. 1, (1958).

4. 369 U.S. 186, (1962).

5. 372 U.S. 335, (1963).

6. 376 U.S. 254, "Proceedings II," Transcript of Oral Arguments, p. 1.

7. Ibid., p. 30.

8. Ibid., p. 31.

9. Ibid., p. 32.

10. Ibid.

11. Ibid., p. 34.

12. Ibid., p. 35.

13. Ibid., p. 38.

14. Ibid.

15. Ibid.

16. Ibid., p. 39.

17. Ibid.

18. Ibid., p. 40.

19. Ibid., p. 41.

20. Ibid., p. 44.

21. Ibid., p. 47.

22. Ibid.

23. Ibid., p. 48.

24. Ibid., p. 51.

25. Ibid., p. 55.

26. Ibid., p. 56.

27. Ibid., p. 57.

28. Ibid., p. 58.

29. Ibid., p. 59.

30. Ibid., p. 61.

31. Ibid., p. 62.

32. Ibid., p. 65.

33. Ibid., p. 67.

34. Ibid., p. 68.

35. Ibid., p. 69.

36. Ibid., p. 76.

37. Ibid., p. 78.

38. Ibid., p. 81.

39. Ibid., p. 83.

40. Kim Isaac Eisler, *A Justice for All: William Brennan, Jr., and the Decisions That Transformed America* (New York: Simon & Schuster, 1993), p. 186.

41. Leon Friedman and Fred Israel, *The Justices of the United States Supreme Court, 1789–1963: Their Lives and Major Opinions* (New York: R. R. Bowker, 1969), p. 2860.

42. Charles Curtis and Shirley Abrahamson, "William Joseph Brennan, Jr.," in Hall, p. 88.

43. Eisler, p. 190.

44. Ibid., p. 187.

45. Bob Woodward and Scott Armstrong, *The Brethren: Inside the Supreme Court* (New York: Simon & Schuster, 1979), p. 46.

46. Ibid.

47. Eisler, p. 190.

48. Anthony Lewis, *Make No Law: The Sullivan Case and the First Amendment* (New York: Random House, 1991), p. 182.

49. *New York Times* v. *Sullivan,* 376 U.S. 254, p. 273.

50. Ibid., p. 289.

51. Ibid., p. 276.

52. Ibid., p. 278.

53. Ibid., p. 269.

54. Ibid., p. 270.

55. Ibid., pp. 271–272.

56. Ibid., p. 279.

57. Ibid., pp. 279–280.

Chapter 6. The Impact of the *Times* Decision

1. Anthony Lewis, "High Court Curbs Public Officials in Libel Actions," *The New York Times*, March 10, 1964, p. 1.

2. Ibid., p. 23.

3. "Free Speech and Free People," editorial, *The New York Times*, March 10, 1964, p. 36.

4. "4 in Suit to Open Restitution Fight," *The New York Times*, March 10, 1964, p. 23.

5. Ibid.

6. Harry Kalven, Jr., "*The New York Times* Case: A Note on the Central Meaning of the First Amendment," *Supreme Court Review*, 1964, p. 209.

7. Ibid., p. 221.

8. 376 U.S. 254, 282 (1964).

9. Ibid., p. 293.

10. Owen Fiss, "A Life Lived Twice," in Roger Goldman and David Gallen, *Justice William J. Brennan, Jr.: Freedom First* (New York: Carroll and Graf, 1964), p. 110.

11. Frank Warnock, "*The New York Times* Rule: The Awakening Giant of First Amendment Protection," Kentucky Law Journal, 62: 827, 830, 1967.

12. Lewis Green, "*The New York Times* Rule: Judicial Overkill," *Villanova Law Review*, 12:735, 1967.

13. Geoffrey Stone, "*New York Times Co. v. Sullivan*," in Kermit Hall, ed., *The Oxford Companion to the Supreme Court of the United States* (New York: Oxford University Press, 1992), p. 586.

14. Ibid., p. 587.

15. Ibid.

16. Rhoda Blumberg, *Civil Rights: The 1960s Freedom Struggle* (Boston: Twayne Publishers, 1991), p. 111.

17. *Garrison* v. *Louisiana,* 379 U.S. 64, 1964.

18. Ibid., p. 77.

19. Clifton Lawhorne, *The Supreme Court and Libel* (Carbondale, Ill.: Southern Illinois University Press), 1981, p. 35.

20. *Associated Press* v. *Walker,* 381 U.S. 130, (1967).

21. *Curtis Publishing Co.* v. *Butts,* 388 U.S. 130 (1967).

22. *Thompson* v. *St. Amant,* 184 So. 2d 314 (1966).

23. *Thompson* v. *St. Amant,* 196 So. 2d 255 (1967).

24. *St. Amant* v. *Thompson,* 390 U.S. 727 (1968).

25. Ibid.

26. Ibid.

27. Ibid.

28. 418 U.S. 323, (1974).

29. Ibid.

30. Ibid.

31. Ibid.

32. Ibid.

33. Ibid.

34. Ibid.

35. Ibid.

36. Ibid.

37. Ibid.

38. Ibid.

39. Norman Rosenberg, "Libel," in Hall, p. 503.

40. Sam Howe Verhovek, "Turf Was Cattlemen's, but Jury Was Winfrey's," *The New York Times,* February 27, 1998, p. A10.

41. Rodney Smolla, *Suing the Press* (New York: Oxford University Press, 1986), pp. 80–99, 164, 199–237.

Glossary

amicus curiae—Someone who is not a party to a lawsuit but who has a point of view for the court to consider.

brief—Written legal arguments presented by the parties to a lawsuit. They are written to persuade the court of a particular position.

civil suits—Actions in court under noncriminal law. Such lawsuits are usually to recover money, to stop someone who is causing an injury, or to decide someone's rights. Unless a party ignores a judge's order, no one is sent to jail in a civil suit.

concurring opinion—An opinion written by a judge who agrees with the decision of the court but disagrees with the reasons for the decision.

court—Judge or judges who sit and listen to arguments or write decisions are called "the court."

criminal trial—The hearing of evidence presented by a lawyer for the government before a judge and, most of the time, before a jury, who decide whether or not a person accused of a crime is guilty and should be jailed or fined.

defendant—The party (or person) in a lawsuit who is being sued. The other party claims to have been wronged by the defendant. A defendant in a criminal case is the person accused of the crime.

dissenting opinion—An opinion written by a judge who disagrees with the opinion of a majority of the court.

double jeopardy—Being tried more than once for the same crime. It is prohibited by the Fifth Amendment.

First Amendment—The constitutional protection for freedom of speech, religion, and the press.

Fourteenth Amendment—Adopted in 1868 to grant citizenship and protect the rights of freedmen. It contains a clause prohibiting the states from depriving any person of life, liberty, or property without "due process of law."

incorporation—The process by which most of the Bill of Rights (first ten amendments to the Constitution) are applied to the states as well as to the federal government.

libel—A false published statement that damages a person's reputation.

malice—Wrongful intent. In libel suits, it is the "reckless disregard of the truth" in a published statement or the deliberate harming of someone's reputation.

negligence—Not exercising proper care, as ordinarily required.

opinion—A written explanation of a judge's decision discussing the legal precedents and the reasoning of the court.

oral argument—An opportunity for the parties to discuss their case with the court. Lawyers answer questions from the court and explain why their party should win.

ordinary damages—Money awarded by the court to a person who was libeled, to make up for an injury to his reputation.

plaintiff—The person or group of people who begin a lawsuit claiming they have been wronged by the defendant.

precedent—All the prior decisions on an issue that is presently before a court. The court is supposed to decide a case in a way that is consistent with previous decisions.

punitive damages—Money awarded to a person who was libeled with malice, or to make an example of the libeler.

sedition—Speech or actions inciting to a rebellion or a breach of public order.

Seventh Amendment—The constitutional right to trial by jury in civil cases (when the "value in controversy" exceeds twenty dollars). The jury's decision is generally final.

Further Reading

Blumberg, Rhoda L. *Civil Rights: The 1960s Struggle*. Boston: Twayne, 1991.

Branch, Taylor. *Parting the Waters: America in the King Years, 1954–1963*. New York: Simon & Schuster, 1988.

Eisler, Kim Isaac. *A Justice for All: William Brennan, Jr., and the Decisions That Transformed America*. New York: Simon & Schuster, 1993.

Fireside, Harvey, and Sarah Betsy Fuller. *Brown v. Board of Education: Equal Schooling for All*. Springfield, N.J.: Enslow Publishers, Inc., 1994.

Forer, Lois G. *A Chilling Effect: The Mounting Threat of Libel and Invasion of Privacy Actions to the First Amendment*. New York: W. W. Norton, 1987.

Garrow, David J. *Bearing the Cross: Martin Luther King, Jr., and the Southern Christian Leadership Conference*. New York: William Morrow, 1986.

Halberstam, David. *The Fifties*, New York: Villard, 1993.

Hopkins, W. Wat. *Mr. Justice Brennan and Freedom of Expression*. New York: Praeger, 1991.

Labunski, Richard. *Libel and the First Amendment: Legal History and Practice in Print and Broadcasting*. New Brunswick, N.J.: Transaction Publishers, 1989.

Lewis, Anthony. *Make No Law: The Sullivan Case and the First Amendment*. New York: Random House, 1991.

Lucas, Eileen. *Civil Rights: The Long Struggle*. Springfield, N.J.: Enslow Publishers, Inc., 1996.

Rosenkranz, E. Joshua, and Bernard Schwarz. *Reason and Passion: Justice Brennan's Enduring Influence*. New York: W. W. Norton, 1997.

Schuman, Michael A. *Martin Luther King, Jr.: Leader for Civil Rights.* Springfield, N.J.: Enslow Publishers, Inc., 1996.

Schraff, Anne. *Coretta Scott King: Striving for Civil Rights.* Springfield, N.J.: Enslow Publishers, Inc., 1997.

Sitkoff, Harvard. *The Struggle for Black Equality, 1954–1992.* New York: Hill & Wang, 1993.

Smolla, Rodney A. *Suing the Press.* New York: Oxford University Press, 1986.

Internet Addresses:

Introduction to Freedom of Speech and Libel Laws
<http://muu.lib.hel.fi/mcspotlight/issues/freedom/index.html>

Pen American Center: Freedom to Write—
Tighter California State Libel Law
<http://pen.org/>

Oprah Airs Her Beef
<http://eonline.com/News/Items/0,1,2488,00.html>

United States Supreme Court Libel Cases
(alphabetical listing)
<http://www.law.newcastle.edu.au/teaching/media/suplib.htm>

Index

127